# Why Strong Women Struggle

How to Win the Battle in Your Private, Professional, and Spiritual Life

By
Gessy Martinez

Aspire and Reach for More, LLC.
Austin, Texas

Gessy Martinez

**Why Strong Women Struggle**
How to Win the Battle in Your Private, Professional, and Spiritual Life

The information in this book is designed to provide helpful information on the subjects discussed. This book is not meant to be used to diagnose or treat any medical or mental health condition. For diagnosis or treatment of any medical problem consult your own medical or mental health professional. The publisher and author are not responsible for any state that may require medical supervision and are not liable for any damages or negative consequences from any treatment, action, application or preparation, to any person reading or following the information in this book.

Neither the publisher nor the individual author(s) shall be liable for any physical, psychological, emotional, financial, or commercial damages, including, but not limited to, special, incidental, consequential or other damages. Resources are provided for informational purposes only and do not constitute an endorsement of any websites or resources. Readers should be aware that the websites and resource contact information listed in this book may change.

Although I am a licensed professional counselor, I am not your counselor. Reading this book does not create a patient-client relationship between us. This book should not be used as a substitute for mental health services of a competent mental health professional credentialed and authorized to practice in your state or country.

This publication is prohibited from reproduction, stored in a retrieval system, or transmitted in whole or in part, in any form or by any means, electronic, mechanical, photocopying, recording, or otherwise without prior written permission of Aspire and Reach for More, LLC.

Copyright © 2011, 2016, 2017 by Gessy Martinez
All Rights Reserved.
Published by Aspire and Reach for More, LLC.
ISBN Number 978-0-9746939-6-5

## Dedications

I thank God for the opportunity to experience and know the power of the life changing relationship in Christ!

My children, you make me brave! When you look at my life, I want you to know that nothing is impossible for you. Dream a bigger dream, love God, yourself, and others. Do what you love and make a difference in the lives of others in the process.

To my friends thank you for the daily encouragement, prayer, and support.

To my clients with each interaction, you have led me to ask more questions to search deeper and grow as a teacher and counselor. Thank you.

| | |
|---|---|
| **THE TITLE MATCH** | 7 |
| **ROUND ONE  PRIVATE LIFE** | 7 |
| **RELATIONSHIPS** | 12 |
| **STRUGGLING WITH LIES** | 13 |
| **STRUGGLING BECAUSE OF WRONG CHOICES** | 18 |
| **STRUGGLING WITH WAITING** | 23 |
| **STRUGGLING WHEN SEX IS YOUR WEAPON** | 29 |
| **STRUGGLING TO KEEP UP APPEARANCES** | 34 |
| **STRUGGLING WITH WANTING & WANING** | 41 |
| **STRUGGLING WHEN LEFT UNLOVED** | 43 |
| **ROUND TWO  THE FIGHT FOR YOUR HOPES, DREAMS, AND CAREER** | 46 |
| **STRUGGLING TO SEIZE THE DAY** | 47 |
| **STRUGGLING WITH LACK OF TIME** | 50 |
| **STRUGGLING WITH STARTING OVER** | 53 |
| **STRUGGLING WITH CONFUSION AND COMPARISON** | 56 |
| **STRUGGLING TO STAY YOUR LANE, YOUR GIFTING** | 59 |
| **STRUGGLING TO NOT FOLLOW, THE HERD** | 69 |
| **STRUGGLING WITH OPPORTUNITIES AND RISK** | 72 |
| **STRUGGLING TO USE TIME EFFECTIVELY** | 75 |

| | |
|---|---:|
| **STRUGGLING WITH WHEN AND HOW TO LISTEN** | 78 |
| **STRUGGLING WITH LACK OF CLARITY** | 81 |
| **STRUGGLING TO WIN WITH THE HAND YOU'RE DEALT** | 84 |
| **STRUGGLING WITH FEELING UNSATISFIED** | 86 |
| **ROUND THREE SPIRITUAL LIFE** | 89 |
| **STRUGGLING TO CELEBRATE SOLO** | 91 |
| **STRUGGLING TO GET UP FROM THE HOSPITAL BED** | 95 |
| **STRUGGLING TO FEEL VALUED AND VALIDATED** | 98 |
| **STRUGGLING TO KNOW THEIR WORTH** | 100 |
| **STRUGGLING WITH LONELINESS** | 104 |
| **STRUGGLING NOT JUST MAKE IT, BE VICTORIOUS** | 109 |
| **STRUGGLING WITH LACK OF HOPE** | 112 |
| **STRUGGLING WITH THE ENEMY IN ME** | 117 |
| **STRUGGLING TO FACE YOUR FEARS** | 119 |
| **STRUGGLING LET GO OF VICTIM MENTALITY** | 123 |
| **STRUGGLING TO KNOW WHO YOU ARE** | 127 |
| **STRONG WOMEN WIN** | 129 |

Why Strong Women Struggle is written to help you identify the reasons, causes, and triggers that lead to positive or harmful behavior. When you recognize patterns or ways of thinking, then you can begin to change the behavior and get different results. Reading this book will help you explore "why you do what you do" and how to begin to change the unproductive thinking and actions that cause you to struggle. You will see in the stories, reminders of women you may know who are strong yet struggle in different areas.

Why Strong Women Struggle is meant to be a conversation starter, it is intended to provoke examination and cause you to think about your life and your choices in a different way. It is meant to be a breath of fresh air for those of us who struggle and feel as if there is no one in the world like them. You are not alone, and your struggle is shared by many other strong women. In this book, we are on the journey together, despite all the resources, experience, and training we all have areas of struggle for understanding and mastery.

I want you to win in your private life and bring balance to your public persona.

Successfully Yours,
Gessy Martinez

# The Title Match

**Round One
Private Life**

The biggest fight you will have in life is between the real you privately, professionally and your public persona. Learning how to reign in your public image before it controls or destroys your private and spiritual life is one of the ways to become successful and satisfied. If you have a habit that is hindering your success until you confront the dysfunction, you will not conquer it. The goal is to get the giant persona back to a manageable size and to deal with the causes of our struggles. In the end, by facing and conquering, you can win in every area of life.

For many of us, the battle between what you do and who you are is a daily occurrence. One example, you are kind and caring, but after being mistreated and disappointed by others, you act in ways that viewed as mean, cold or uncaring. You want a healthy relationship but choose men that almost guarantee unhealthy exchanges. Find your self-wanting one thing but making choices that produce the opposite. To gain an understanding of the why, begin by looking at areas where the struggles stem. Your private life often pays the consequence and bears the burden to make your public persona what it has become.

As a strong woman, you could struggle in your private life because of:

- Living to please others.

- Being addicted to a substance.
- Worried about not being in control of your family.
- Being angry all the time and not knowing why.
- Feeling sick of it all and wanting something different.
- Having to keep secrets that are tearing up your soul.
- Never thinking you are good enough or that you deserve the best.
- Not saying no to family members who take and never give.
- Being limited by someone who uses you as a showpiece, beautiful and ignored.
- Trying to be authentic, yet everyone wants you to be what they want.
- Your life is in chaos and spiritual foundation shaky.
- Married to a man who is a batterer, abuser or womanizer.

As a strong woman, you could struggle in your professional life as a result of:

- Giving up your life to make someone else dream come true.

- Successful and admired in business but your kids hate you.
- Living in fear of being exposed to others as incompetent or unqualified.
- Fighting for so long against the odds that you cannot rest or enjoy the success.
- Being an influential figure and left with no one to turn to when they hurt you.
- Working so much that you have lost your close friends.
- Fear that you can't trust anyone around you.
- Being a barracuda in business, surpassing your friends, and now abandoned by them.

As a strong woman, you could struggle in spiritually because of:

- Disappointment by a parent or spiritual figure.
- Once I believed then tragedy shook my faith.
- Misperceptions of God's role in your life.
- Mistreatment by someone in the church.
- Wanting relationship but finding only more religion.
- Feeling forgotten, abandoned by the ones meant to care for you.
- Growing up without freedom to express or deny faith.
- Not understanding how faith can work in your life.

- Missing role models who balance faith with professional and financial success.

Now that we have identified some of the common reasons we struggle in our private, professional and spiritual life. Let us go deeper in why struggle privately and professionally and how we win this fight in every area. In the pages following this book are designed and separated by specific areas and the struggles within those topics.

# Relationships

We begin with a look at the biggest area of our lives, relationships. How we relate to others in our personal lives will determine the depth of joy or the lack thereof in our professional life. Our relationships from birth to the end of our life shape who we are, who we become and how other people perceive us. Through our relationships, we learn about ourselves.

There is a saying "if you look at someone's friends you will have a good indication of the type of person they are." This is an inaccurate statement because in some professions you may have people in your life perceived as having a relationship with you when it is more superficial than intimate. This next topic covers the people who you have chosen to be in a close relationship with.

## Struggling with lies

**"I gave him everything he wanted, and he still left.** The relationship began like most, fun, exciting and full of promise. We were pursuing our careers goals. It felt magical we were young, spontaneous and felt like just the two of us existed in this whole world. Our friends would tease us "Sarah and Sam the perfect couple". It seemed so right that I settled in and acted like a married couple. I never had a real commitment I told myself I didn't need it, hey; I know of married couples who do not relate as well as me and Sam, So why bother? We were happy, and that is all that counts.

A year went by, and small nuances started to creep up, Sam didn't like how I did the laundry, so I changed and did the laundry exactly how he likes it. He later complained a little more saying he felt unsupported, so I gave him all my attention and stroked his ego as often as he needed it.

Later he complained about not liking the way I cook so I took a cooking class and tried to cook better. Now I was managing my career, home responsibilities while changing my look, habits, and even preferences to cater to him. This worked on the surface for a few more years.

Then affection got less, the sex was down to none, and he is always busy or unhappy when I'm around. I was what he wanted, the ideal "wifey," and both of us were unhappy.

I would go over and over in my head it must be something I am not doing? What is it? I would do anything for him if I only knew what it was?

Meanwhile, I was becoming angry, and feeling rejected and lonely. I try harder and harder to connect with him when I could get his attention; he just became meaner. Then, like a gut punch in the stomach, he packs up and leaves. Then one day he left and disappeared from all our social media and stop answering my calls. Sam left me with years of my life turned into a blur of complacency, and compromise. The very thing I was afraid of happening has happened, he left without explanation or an affair. He is gone, and I'm left to discover who I am and what just happened.

The situation:
- Sarah gave Sam everything he asked for, and he left.
- Sarah was searching for what went wrong by asking how can I fix it; how do I get him back?
- Sarah was in a co-dependent relationship.
- Sarah and Sam were in denial about the true problem in their relationship.

Sarah is facing a revelation that in giving Sam exactly what he thought he wanted or thought he needed, she forgot something. What Sam needed was the real, authentic Sarah. Sometimes the very qualities that attract someone to you are the first things changed when things appear to be going wrong. When conflict comes, it is time, to be honest and not to retreat emotionally.

Sarah's need to please Sam, take on the caretaker role and not reinforce her boundaries or express her needs to silence her voice and give Sam control. This created an environment that allowed problems with intimacy, communication and painful emotions to develop.

Conflict comes desiring to be resolved by those entangled in it. If a compromise is reached only for the sake of temporary peace and not resolution, then someone is often left as the losing party on the other side of the compromise. Compromise is only fair if both parties are ready to listen, validate each other and demonstrate respect.

We often seek temporary band-aids to stop the arguing because we are tired of fighting and not because we want resolution. We need to fix what needs fixing. The problem with band-aids is that they fall off, without much resistance. Band-aids last for a very short time; the bleeding may stop, but the wound does not always heal properly.

Relationships built on compromise, complacency, or "need to please" are susceptible to cracks in the foundation and breaking apart. They cannot resist the pressure of strong temptation, difficulties, and the time factor. Like a house built on a poor foundation that in time deteriorates from the pounding by forces of nature. Relationships not reinforced by truth, when tested will deteriorate because it is not built on something solid. You can't pretend or live a lie forever. Our true nature is revealed with time, and then conflict ensues.

Selfish people get tired or bored of getting their way, often seeking some constraints and resistance to help them deal with a trait they are not proud of. A man wants a challenge; he wants the strong woman he fell in love with, the strong woman he pursued and had to work to get. Never lose or suppress who you are becoming what someone else thinks they want. Remember most people take years to know what they want. This is because we tend to choose a mate who will perpetuate some of the very habits we need to change.

A strong woman is like a muscle, with each struggle and resistance she grows stronger. She constantly must develop and evolve mentally and emotionally to stay strong. Over time she can weaken in some areas, yet easily brought back on track with the right thinking and inner work.

# Struggling Because of Wrong Choices

## "They are either Married or a Mess!

"Why is it that the type of men I attract are either married or a mess?" Are you finding yourself constantly attracting married men? It may be the messages or signals you are not paying attention to or the method you use to choose a man that is causing the problem.

*How we find the married.*

Your criteria for Mr. Right may look like a resume for a married man. Most married men give a sense of security, maturity, and patience. When you are with them, your guard may be down because you do not feel a sense of having to play cat and mouse. There is less overt flirtation, less pressure and you can be yourself which can be a pleasing experience. There exists the freedom of not having to be on alert, or deal with the sexual tension that sometimes arises between singles.

When you get involved with a married man, the attention they give you makes you feel at the moment, as if no one else in the world matters. They are polite, kind, always genuinely seem to care. They will comfort, encourage, and do their very best to please you in every way (especially sexually). It seems like an adventure at the beginning with the secret meetings, and you almost never hear of the spouse and children. It seems as good as having your favorite piece of chocolate stored in a secret place there for your pleasure on a bad day, a lonely moment or an emotional low. Like the stashed away chocolate sooner or later what you had in secret leaves evidence in the open for all to see. Its effects are like weight gain, hard to lose and it takes more time to push away and resist than it did to gain.

Getting involved and staying involved with these types of men can kill your self-esteem; place your life and career at risk. Your life and health are at risk because the man cheating with you may have more than one mistress and opening the possibilities to sexually transmitted diseases. An affair can lead to a financial loss if it's with a client or co-worker. It can also damage your reputation and take away from your ability to perform at the workplace should it get out of control. It can also hurt not only the children of the other party but your own as well, upon being found out. These types of forbidden relationships have potential consequences that can reach into generations and at the very least cause, lengthy court battles should a child result from an affair.

### *How we find the messy situations*

We send messages to others by how we carry ourselves, how we speak about ourselves to others. We can portray confidence one minute then in the same interaction show desperation by sharing something inappropriate. We can say we are not in a rush to get serious, yet we see the guy three times in the first week and call on the phone every day twice a day. We talk about wanting a long-term loving relationship yet have sex on the first date. We can say "I am over my ex" yet many conversations lead back to the ex and what they did. We tell ourselves I am not going to get involved with men with issues anymore, yet we expect to find Mr. Right in the bar, through jail pen pals or from the office pool.

We tell ourselves I am worthy to be loved and treated with respect. We are excited by the guy who seems arrogant, disrespectful and easily angered. His arrogance seems like confidence because he won't take any mess, yet later on, that turns into refusing to listen to you. He is aggressive, and that looks attractive until you get a glimpse of it out of control. Now you understand how he could have ended up in jail. We find ourselves attracted to someone who needs us. They have a problem, and we are strong and intelligent enough to handle it for them. We tell ourselves reassuring statements like:

"with my help, he could be successful";
"no one understands him but me";
"others did him wrong";

"It's not his fault; it's the tramps he has been with."

These are messages we hear and tell ourselves right before taking on a relationship with someone who has a lot of unresolved issues. Some issues that we find ourselves trying to resolve or help them heal through are:

* Past bad marriage which ended resentfully and he owes child support while fighting with the ex-wife over visitation.
* A pending divorce which is ugly and ongoing, costing him money, time and peace.
* Having spent time in jail and he cannot find employment, and it's been two years and many training schools later with no steady results.
* A man who would make the GQ magazine cover, he reveals you are his one true love, and by the way, he has HIV.
* He has grown children who are extremely manipulative, financially needy and will wrestle or scheme for their father's attention.
* He is showing signs of addiction, but when you express concern, he tells you it's under control and not as bad as you are making out to be.

These statements are not meant to put down men who are dealing with these issues or to say you can't find a good man dealing with the above challenges. What is important to prepare yourself and keep in mind as a strong woman are you ready to handle:

1) The possibilities of these issues taking years to resolve?

2) Are you emotionally prepared, if you do not have the full attention of your mate or all your needs met because of the issues?

3) Are you ready to sacrifice career, your dream, money and time to help your mate resolve these issues?

4) Are you ready to deal with you mate becoming discouraged or fearful and never working on an issue that may affect your family and future?

These questions are to help you deal with the "what if?" What if you get involved, and you do not get what you expect? Are you still willing to believe, work and stay committed to a man who is not on a mission or with a mission but has become the mission himself? If you decided to pursue the relationship, do it with your eyes wide open to the truth about the emotional work, time and energy, it would take. Be realistic about your expectations, what you hope to get and what you can give to this relationship.

## Struggling with Waiting

If you have found yourself saying "what if Mr. Right never comes?" you could be in operating in emergency mode. Have you ever seen an ambulance with its lights blaring through the streets, running through the red, yellow and green lights driving straight past everyone, breaking all the laws of traffic to rush to their destination? We are equally driven and urgent in pursuing a mate when it seems like our time is running out.

The biological clock seems to be running out, and you are feeling the pressure. On the made-up list of success indicators, you have to check off is a husband, listed as the next achievement on the list. Your friends are getting married, all causing you to go into anxiety, fear and a search for Mr. Right. Like the ambulance blazing forward ignoring all the red lights indicating to stop, and rest or the yellow saying slow down, to enjoy the journey. You will even past the green saying it is safe to go here instead of choosing to go another direction. You ignore it all focused on getting to the wedding chapel as soon as possible.

You are expecting in this mad frantic pace and with all this pressure to make a sound decision and choose the right mate. You expect in a time of desperation and loneliness to choose someone with your values and dreams. Have you ever been extremely hungry and found yourself reaching for the nearest donut or anything just to fill the hunger and stop the pain. This poor decision making happens in dating and choosing a mate in a rush by trying to meet some preset deadline or avoid the pain of loneliness.

If you have ever had a cake made from scratch that took time and had fresh, natural ingredients and then a cake made from a box in 30 minutes you will taste a significant difference. The difference between a partner you have waited for and chosen during a time of contentment, peace, and abundance can be just as significant. When we race in desperation mode, marrying or committing to Mr. Wrong, we will spend more years frustrated and now entangled. When making such an important decision as who to marry you want to be in the best possible condition emotionally, spiritually and financially to avoid making the wrong choice.

We rush because we view our "pickings as slim." As if all the men in the world are taken so you should just settle. You have more options than what is presented to you. Your choices may seem to be few because the reach of your fishing net and the place you are casting from are too small. Your net may be limited to your neighborhood, your church, club or favorite hangout.

The reach of your net is maybe limited to your financial status, ethnicity or country. What if you are in the United States and your Mr. Right is in Europe. What if he had every attribute on your list but was Asian, and you are Italian or Republican, and you are a Democratic? What if he was a truck driver and you are a corporate executive. How wide is your fishing net? Are you willing to look beyond your list to someone who has everything you need but not all you want? God may be sending you someone you need, who does not have a degree but has a strong work ethic, smart, loving and kind. You want Mr. Corporate America who is emotionally unavailable, selfish, and needy.

Choose a mate keeping in mind one day the degree will fade, your achievements are forgotten, and your breast sagging. You may need someone to comb your hair, read you a story, and visit you in the hospital. Old age will come, and you want someone you can grow old alongside not someone who will jump ship at the slightest sign of imperfection.

Ask yourself these questions of the one on your list:
* Can you see yourself growing with this person?
* What will you talk about in old age?
* Does he have enough character to demonstrate moral values to your kids?

* Could you endure caring for him if a sudden accident left him without the use of his limbs?
* If he was unable to do what he does now or make the same amount of money, how do you think he would handle it?
* Would he still find you attractive after weight gain?

To choose right, you will have to separate your wants from your needs. How do you separate your wants from your needs? Your wants will lead you to desire the ideal man in the ideal conditions. Your needs lead you to desire someone who will help you become a better person. The person you need will be the one who is not impressed by your accomplishments but can tell you the truth about your behavior and attitude. You need a partner who will be honest, loving, faithful and consistent.

We usually want those who say the right things truthful or not, who appease and please. A partner who is impressed by your persona and ask very little emotionally from you in the relationship. You need someone who can keep you from extremes and remind you of what is important. Someone who can encourage you to stay humble, and allow you to be emotionally naked and unashamed in their presence during times of intimacy. To reach your potential in marriage and life and it may require someone you do not always agree with but always love.

### *What is negotiable in looking for Mr. Right?*

The negotiable items depend on what you value and are priorities in marriage. It could be income level; if you make a comfortable living salary and your partner's income would be a bonus, then the salary is negotiable.

A negotiable is maybe having or not having children, for example, if you have a child, a relationship with someone who has a child can be a negotiable issue.

If you love children and having one is important, then this becomes non-negotiable with your mate. If you are not able to care for children or do not want children, that should be non-negotiable.

If he has everything you need and want but is a different culture that may be negotiable, depending on your extended family relations. Your "non-negotiables" based on principles, not preferences.

The "negotiables" depend on many factors such as your tolerance level, your belief in the strength of the relationship, your ability to look ahead and see the individual's potential. It also factors in your ability to look beyond the physical and incorporate the spiritual principles of the person. It requires that you be realistic; do not require Mr. Perfect when you are Ms. Issues.

*Ask yourself I am unrealistic and uncompromising?*

Be honest about what you bring to the table and what you have to offer someone. Some women come to a relationship, in debt and want a man with good credit and money. It is unrealistic to want someone to do for you what you must do for yourself. It is not your partner's responsibility to rescue you, and that expectation is a sure way to start a relationship with problems. Enter into the relationship with as much to offer as you are requiring.

The questions for you to explore and answer are:
*What are my priorities in a relationship?*
*What are nonnegotiable in my relationship?*
*What do I bring to a relationship?*

# Struggling When Sex is Your Weapon

**Love, Power, and Sex**

If you are a survivor of sexual abuse, then sex was once used as a weapon against you, a tool used to tear away your innocence. Something that kept you attached to someone in secrecy and fear. Predators of sexual assault and abuse used fear, shame, guilt, manipulation, deception, and violence against their victims.

Each survivor deals with the pain of their abuse or assault differently. There are three ways some survivors can manifest how they express or deal with the trauma covered in the next few pages. The three ways it can manifest are through behaviors meant to gain power, self-denial or inflict punishment.

When sex is used to gain power, it may seem like a game of give and take, take and take more. Sex may have been used to control you and make you do things that embarrassed you, things that may have left you with nightmares, anxieties, and fear of sudden disaster or being victimized again. Now you have taken the weapon used against you, and now you handle it, like a sword you use it against others.

These are the thoughts of someone where sex has become a game, *"I tease you, you chase me, I make you sweat, drool, beg and then lust. I got you paying my bills, buying what I want, and occasionally I throw you the best steak you ever had. I give you something to brag about and have made you believe that no one could satisfy me like you do. Meanwhile, in my heart, I am disgusted, angry and can't wait for you just get off me. I despise how you allow me to do whatever I want and can't have the backbone to say no to me. I need you to feed my ego and pay for what other men have done to me. They told me once I was the worst type of woman. I have been called a whore and every other name in the book. I fought those lies for a while; then one day just began to act out the very names they called me. I became good at it; I turned heads of men and made the women wonder; now I am sick of it all. I hate what I do and who I have become but letting it go it too hard. It would mean letting go of the finer things I have become accustomed to during this relationship.*

The questions for you to explore and answer are:
*Do you see your in this scenario?*
*How does this way of relating serve you?*
*How does it hinder you?*

The game of love, power, and sex can meet the unfilled need, release the anger or provide temporary relief. It can numb you to the pain of the past or make you feel vindicated and powerful. Although you were never able to get the revenge you felt due; now every man pays for it, everyone regardless of their potential is entitled to share your pain. Therefore you distribute emotional pain, distress, and revenge without conscience or regret because the pain you carry is so great. The humiliation you suffered was so bad; it does not compare to what you require of your partners. You have left behind you a trail of broken hearts, unfulfilled promises, and enough returned engagement rings to stock a jewelry store counter.

To stop playing the game of using sex as power would mean leaving yourself vulnerable. Possibly being in relationships without a familiar tool, even when the tool it is a double edge sword. To stop would mean dealing with loneliness and going back to feeling powerless. Getting out of the game will mean dealing with emotions you have buried. For some the unhealed expression of their pain is the need for revenge, control, releasing anger and to regain sexual power in the relationship. To meet this need, some will engage in self-harm by using sex as a tool or weapon.

The questions for you to explore and answer are:
*When you play this game are you getting what you need?*
*How long can you carry on this type of relationships?*
*How many partners left wounded will it take to make up what happened to you?*
*Do you have power outside the bedroom?*

Strong women may appear powerful because they lead in the game of sex and power. They are destroying their true power each time they engage in acts and relationships that violate their bodies, self-esteem, and purpose. You were not created to be used like a dirty rag or a weapon; your purpose is greater; your worth is unmatched and of great value to God.

## Sex, Powerlessness, and Self-denial

Some survivors can manifest in dealing with the pain and trauma through self-denial. A violation can lead to a sense of powerlessness and not being in control of your body, sexual desire or expression. To regain or maintain power, feel in control and safe some will deny their sexual desires and freedom within a marriage. This is shutting down and closing parts of their heart, mind, and body to experiencing intimacy in a safe, loving relationship.

These are the thoughts of someone denying themselves the right to be intimate and enjoy sex with their partner, *"I love my husband, but I haven't told him what happened to me. Sometimes during intimacy, I shut down, or m mind goes somewhere else. I love my husband, but I don't really need or want sex. I know it makes him happy, and I participate but its to see a smile on his face. Sometimes he does things I don't like, but I remember that I am a wife and this is part of the role. I wonder if he can tell. I wonder if he knows. I'm scared to tell him about in case he thinks it's my fault or asks questions I don't want to answer. No matter how much he tells me, I don't feel beautiful. He never asked me what I like, so I don't tell him. I'm not sure what I like really when it something feels like it would make me happy or feel good, I shut down, I think about other things. I am afraid to enjoy sex because I was made to feel bad about it."*

This lack of intimacy and self-denial grows when you don't share your thoughts, likes, dislikes or fears related to sex and intimacy with your partner. You are physically present and participating, your partner thinks you are enjoying sex, but during the act, you move into a routine and perform but don't allow yourself to enjoy the emotional and physical connection. You even turn off the lights and won't let your partner see you naked or exposed in any way. There is the role you play and hidden beneath is the real you, protected and afraid many years after the hurt took place.

Questions to explore:
*How much has this behavior cost me?*
*What can I gain from being honest and allow my spouse in?*
*What are some safe ways I can start build trust & intimacy?*

You may ask yourself why you should stop using what has worked for you up until now?

Both expressions of pain whether playing a game of control or self-denial are harmful to your mind, body and can enable further trauma and pain.

# Struggling to Keep up Appearances

I am living with an image

*When we first met I was impressed by his command of a room; the man is the stuff of legends. Books are written about men like him, admired, respected, loved and feared by those who encounter him. His passion for his work causes you to choose sides, and trust me you want to be on his when all is said and done. I love reading his bio it is the stuff Hollywood movies are made of, rising out of hard times, hard life and made in an industry once closed off to people from his side of the tracks. I love the access his name was able to acquire, women envy our relationship. We were powerful and attractive as a couple. In public, he treats me like a queen in private as his personal dumping station. I see him out of the spotlight when everyone has gone home; he is scared, plagued by nightmares, unsure and dependent on meds to bring him up and meds to take him down. I got what I wanted and some things I did not bargain for with this relationship. He came with not one but two ex-wives, several children, financial obligations, worries and much more.*

*At times I feel as if I am his security blanket, temporarily meeting a need. He admires my mind yet privately attacks my suggestions, and the public takes credit for them. He says he loves me but will not take me around his family, and I fear he has closed off his most intimate side to me. I feel so alone, yet constantly surrounded by fans, supporters, and people who want something.*

*I can't complain because no one would take me seriously, many want us to fail. I can't cry because then I look weak and the first sign of weakness he is disgusted and attacks. When I am honest and begin to share, he can't take it sees it as me not being happy, wanting too much. Next thing I know, he is gone for hours, sometimes days. I can't leave; I am unofficially married to the man, the mission, the image. I love the perks, the power, and the prestige and even though things are not ideal, I settle. I am hoping to have a child, make my mark on his heart, keep him for good, and penetrate the emotional wall he has up.*

The problem with idols is that because they are manmade, they come with flaws, they must be kept up, cleaned up and need continuous admiration. Idols usually require a sacrifice, and they demand everything and give nothing. You may tell yourself that you do not idolize this man, but a simple test can reveal if you do.

### *Ask yourself these questions:*
- When this person comes around your focus, attitude and demeanor change; do you become guarded and careful with your words?
- Would your friends say that you are a much different person when your partner is not around?
- Do you get tense and nervous about sharing something you think would not be approved by your partner?

- Are you exhausted from taking care and constantly encouraging this person?
- Does this person care for you with at least half of the thoughtfulness and intensity as you do for them?
- When this person is not around, do you find yourself relieved and feeling free?
- Are you afraid of losing this person and do they use this as a threat against you?
- Does this person put you down subtlety, jokingly or in a blunt way?

Be careful about trying to change someone who has deep-rooted issues which they are refusing to deal with, or change, despite the pain. If they do not want to deal with it, they will not want you to force them or try to counsel them into changing. As a strong, intelligent woman who can influence leaders, friends, and others to change you may think "I can make my partner change".

We can at times be overly optimistic, blind or arrogant in this pursuit. Change must come from a desire from the inside to change. Outside circumstances can give rise to the desire for change or even help to propel change. You are very different from your mate, and cannot control when or how it will happen, or know what will work to initiate it. You may think that after having a child together your relationship will be much more intimate and caring, yet the child comes, and he is more distant and selfish than ever. It is important, to be honest, and not place an expectation of change on your mate that is unrealistic.

We tear down idols in our lives when seeing people for who they are, human, with weakness as well as strengths. Even the strong are needy in some area of their lives when they learn to reveal then they can heal. Unless they are willing you cannot make this happen, you cannot force it, and you cannot manipulate it. To try to do this would only bring hurt, disappointment, and rejection.

We tear down idols in our life when we take responsibility for our emotional needs not being met and do not expect life, fame or money or our mate to meet it. Someone else's things may give you access, but it should not define you or limit you only to what they provide.

We tear down idols in our life when we place God first and people under his management and guidance. We tear down idols when we pursue our development and growth. Often what we admire in others are the characteristics we need to birth from within ourselves. If you admire someone's courage and determination, work on building that within yourselves to see your dreams come true. The stronger we become emotionally, the more we will win the admiration of others. As an unintended consequence, they will change how they relate to you.

### *Any man is better than no man*

One of the greatest fears strong women harbor is the fear of being alone. The fear of being alone associated with feeling vulnerable, unwanted and forgotten. We all want to matter; we all need to feel protected. Often the fear of being alone is followed by anxiety attacks and a sick feeling of pending trouble. Your self-confidence begins to wane, and doubt plagues your mind. Some feel the cure for this is someone, anyone. Thinking to themselves "maybe I do not need Mr. Right but Mr. Right now, or Mr. Will do to help with the loneliness."

The danger of settling for anyone less than the best for you lies in the consequences of making that choice. You face the danger of being tied up with Mr. Wrong when Mr. Right may come and go, and you miss the opportunity. Mr. Right cannot be placed in a position that is already taken. If the one you are with is causing warning signs to go off, then you may have to fire him.

Your choices may seem limited because of what you are putting out there during your search. You are doing the seeking when you should be sought after. In our impatience to find someone, we let be known either by actions or choices that we need a man NOW. We are desperate and do not care who knows it. Well, the unfaithful married men and the others who are a mess are out there seeking for someone who is in such a rush that they will not have the time or the right frame of mind to pay attention to the signals.

Moving forward out of deep desperation to fill the bed with a warm body or feel a man's touch we run blindly into the arms of Mister Wrong. Had we waited longer he may have run out of smooth lines, perfect behavior, and exciting thrills to allow us to see cover ups and inconsistencies. By the time we wake up to the truth we find that we have already given up the goods and may have gotten in deeper than we could have imagined; breaking up now means starting the search over again after six months of a whirlwind relationship. For some, it means starting over after finding you are pregnant or getting a call from the wife. Mr. Right Now or Mr. Will Do come with complications and long terms issues that you want to avoid.

When you are facing the urge and time of loneliness, fight to not making a long-term decision based on a temporary need. Urges past if you resist them, times of loneliness are just that moments of time, they will pass if you focus on other things and get busy living and enjoy your life. Learning to enjoy being alone so that when with others the time is fully engaged and well spent.

Questions to explore:
*How much has this behavior cost me?*
*What choices have you made in the past when lonely that you later regretted?*
*Why do you feel pressured?*
*How do I imagine my relationships in the future?*

## Struggling with Wanting & Waning

Being single in a world so driven by sex, sexuality and the pursuit of relations is difficult. You find yourself as a single person dealing with the lack of a significant other being the number one issue plaguing your life. One reason this is a constant issue may be your friends and family members taking every opportunity to ask if there is someone new in your life.

Family members are known for using gathering or holidays to probe with interest for any hint of gossip about your personal life as if they were trying to live vicariously through you. Although you answer either with humor or stern rebuke when you leave them, your heart begins to long for someone. The questions such as "why don't I have someone"; "when will I find the right person," "what is wrong with me that I can't find someone" all swirls around in your mind.

You try to appear to your friends and family as if you do not want or need men. There are times when you are doing great and not thinking about your aloneness. Other times the loneliness and the desire to be touched and held seem so strong that you go right back to a place of desperately wanting and impatient about waiting. Wanting "Mr. Right," or considering

"Mr. Right now" and when the desperation seems too much, you almost admit to being willing for a "Mr. Fixer upper."

Without knowing there is a danger when you are wanting and waiting for a long time to get into a place of waning. Waning is slow decrease in the belief this will turn out good, feeling weaker, doubtful about the decision you made. This is a place of diminished expectation, diminishing joy and almost a sense of hopelessness in this area of your life. Waning decreases your hope and leaves room in your mind to believe things that are not proven fact. It can also cause you to stop striving after the things that matter to you. It has made some stop living with joy and turn their focus to what they lack rather than what they have.

Your singleness will afford opportunities to do things that marriage or relationships hinder. Being single is not forever so instead of spending the time wanting, waiting and waning, go and do, live, try and enjoy. As a single person, you can work on yourself and do the things that would be considered selfish when you are in a relationship.

Questions to explore:

*What have you learned from your past relationships about yourself?*

*How do you deal with relationship disappointments?*

*What is your biggest fear about being alone?*

## Struggling When Left Unloved

The Constant Encourager

You are the constant encourager and now you are wondering "who is left to encourage me or is anyone listening as I try to help?" Encouragers understand that people listen in different ways; some will listen and immediately put your advice to work. Some will listen and fight you on every word said, and advice given; they will seem to hate your idea or act as if you have some other motive behind your response. Do not base the weight of your words on the immediate reactions they produce. Based on your words of encouragement on the results, they bring back.

There are times we must purpose in our mind to encourage ourselves when no one is available to encourage us. I use the word available not in terms of presence but available in terms of emotions. People who are encouragers are optimistic and see the best and the possibilities in every situation. They see opportunity where others see obstacles. The ability to encourage others is a gift; it is powerful and influential. It comes from someone who has a heart for others and can sense when someone needs that extra push.

People who need constant encouragement tend to be pessimistic and unavailable emotionally to help others because they are busy fighting their own battles.

They view themselves as practical therefore always seeing the practical obstacles instead of the probable opportunity. The matching of a pessimist and an optimist is usually a good pairing because of the need for balance and hope in life. When in a relationship with a pessimist you may need other encouraging people to get the boost in confidence or support you need.

The ability to see all the expressions of love around you can help reduce the feelings of being unloved. Take inventory of your relationships and ask the question what ways is this person showing me they care about me? For example, you may have a mother who is not affectionate but is reliable and always calls to check on how you are doing. This may be how your mother expresses love by being available, present and reliable. Your partner may think buying gifts is their expression of love because they don't have time or ability to express love in other ways. Taking inventory can help you see how others show concern, help provide for your needs and prove that you are loved.

The feeling of not being loved may be rooted in feelings of unworthiness, shame, failure or not being good enough. Practicing gratitude for the relationships and connections in your life that are trustworthy, consistent and faithful can help increase feeling connected and loved.

Exercise combating the negative thoughts of rejections, feelings of disregard or anger, with truth. The truth is you are loved, there are people who care about you. The best way to combat a lie is with the truth. There are people in your circle who know you intimately, care about you and genuinely want to see you succeed.

If a past mistake or failure is causing you to distance yourself from loved one, this can cause you to feel unloved and unworthy. It's time to practice kindness, self-forgiveness and self-compassion to rebuild your sense of worth. A mistake can leave you feeling like there is no way to rebound or correct the hurt that might have been caused. It is possible to repair your relationships and bring it back to loving and caring place. It will take forgiving self and others and allowing love to come into your life in many ways. While encouraging others apply that encouragement, kindness and love to yourself first. Daily practice encouraging yourself with positive thoughts and refuel your love tank with affirmations.

Questions to explore:
*When do you feel most loved?*
*How do you encourage yourself when feeling down?*
*Who are the consistent and faithful friends in your life and when was the last time you told them?*

# Round Two
# The fight for your hopes, dreams, and career

This fight is waged against several opponents, lack of resources, internal bouts with low self-confidence, the aging clock, not many mentors, other commitments, the need for safety and assurance. In this round, you can have many opponents in the corner waiting to knock you down one after the other, sometimes in a team attack.

The fuel for this round will come from the very thing you are fighting to birth and preserve. You will get your passion from your dreams your fuel from the hope of seeing them realized. The establishment of your career goals and a clear vision for your life will make you rock solid in the midst of an uncertain world. You are more than what it appears right now. You have potential, vision, creativity, and greatness inside of you waiting to be revealed to the world.

## Struggling to Seize the Day

Today is the best day of your life if you choose to make so. When the day or your emotions start to get out of control, do not give up and call it a loss. Take hold of the day; all is not lost until. Use the time you have left well. Recover the day if it is going badly. You did not get to your to-do list, so the day began the way too early, and it is getting late, and you have not worked on any of your goals. Well do not stop there, begin now late in the day or late in the night to do at least one thing that will help you achieve your goals.

All is not lost, do not live life constantly letting it roll over you and feeling defeated because you cannot get a break. If you pause and change your reaction you can save the day. What happens to some is the day begins with an email, text or phone call (drama) we play into and try to fix it. Then we are off schedule, hurried and if we have people, we are responsible for spending the day reacting and trying to be productive at the same. Our emotions are out of whack, and we are fighting to just get through the day instead of experience and control it.

The disappointment the next day is the regret of not accomplishing what we set out to do, or not honoring our resolutions.

What is factual: you cannot and will not conform to other people's expectations. What other people think matters only to the point that people matter. They should not be able to manipulate or stifle you with their opinions.

Getting control of your day is made easier when you respond accordingly rather than react without thoughtful planning. Give all emergencies a rating and if the true rating is low then keep it as a nonpriority, if high then plan and execute. Place a sign above your computer and a note in your phone saying, "not every emergency is my concern," if it's not life and death, then it can be handled by someone else or at a later time.

Seize the day, by saying no and mean no. You have the right to protect your day and your time. The practice of saying no to others is saying yes to you; yes to what matters most, yes to what can be achieved when you are given the room to focus. Guard your time as if gold and use this precious commodity to accomplish your goals and to prevent a minor crisis in controlling your emotions.

It's your day; your life makes it count to make it profitable. When it comes to your emotions, they will be shaken, but you hold power to still them. In dealing with others, they will demand your attention and try to arrest your time for their benefit as they try nothing matters as much as how you feel about the situation.

Questions to explore:
*What or who is consuming the most of your time?*
*What are interruptions and time wasters you can cut out of your life?*
*Does your priorities and values match in time spent, i.e., value family and spend most of your time with family?*

## Struggling with Lack of Time

How do I start again and what do I do with what I have left? What do you do when you have invested years moving through the corporate web and have given the best of yourself only to find at 50 years old you are now facing layoff? You look outside your company and realize while you were doing everything right and fighting the politics, social and other wars on the inside the game has changed. Contacts you built your reputation with have moved on to other positions and worse other fields. The world is now going global, but you did not have the time, energy or desire to learn another language or take the risk involved. You think I am too old to go back to school and if I did what would I take? I am not the entrepreneur type; I still have children living at home, so what do I do now?

Begin by not panicking, yes, the game may have changed on the surface, but there are still some basic things that do not change. People and the importance of relationships and connections do not change. The foundations that birth industries do not change, methods and systems may change, but the purpose and the goals are still the same. If you are in the banking industry, its purpose is to make money for shareholders by investing the money of account holders does not change.

How this is executed may change for example mutual funds are popular one year, and stocks are popular again the next year. Begin with what you know when looking to see where your skills are most applicable and transferable. Consider working for an industry that complements or is connected to the field you previously worked in. Therefore, you can continue to build on your skills.

Another option is to explore becoming what you always wanted to be, even if it seems that career may not bring in the compensation that you are comfortable with. If you have spent 30 years working in a career field because of the prestige and luxuries, it afforded, the idea of living off of less money is laughable. You are probably thinking to yourself "is she crazy, to give up the income and go back to living on budgets, not being certain if I will make my house and car payment is not realistic for me." Consider the following; it took more than your education to get to where you are now, your skills and talents added greatly to your success.

The same skills and talents that you used to succeed in one industry you can use to help you succeed in another. A winner can be a winner anywhere they are planted because the skills and attitude that it takes to win in one area are transferable to another. An attitude like positivity, optimism, humility, generosity with skills like discipline, communications, relationship, willingness to study and insight can help you win in any arena when applied properly. Say to yourself "I will put one foot in front of the other and begin to explore my options."

Questions to explore:
*How does your past define you?*
*What are your fears about starting over?*
*What are some of your unknown talents and skills?*
*What new skill or ability would you like to learn?*

## Struggling with Starting Over

Starting over in a new job or new career is not easy. Your attitude is crucial in making the experience rewarding. Try to remain optimistic, open to new ideas and a new way of working. Starting over will require that you show aspects of your personality that may have been guarded in the past. In some workplaces, a person who is always smiling and joking is considered not serious and unreliable, in another working environment laughter, smiling and a relaxed demeanor is welcomed and encouraged. You may have previously worked in an environment where casual was the norm, and now you are expected to dress more formal and look as if you command authority and possess money. Take the change as an opportunity to diversify your wardrobe and your perspective of the marketplace.

Learn as much as you can learn and use this new experience to transfer lessons into opportunities for success and furthering your development as an excellent employee. Starting over can be the fresh air you have needed and can awake your spirit while igniting your creativity. We need challenges that can sharpen our skills and make us more effective in the workplace; this is often lacking when you are in a place where you feel you mastered your potential.

Starting over allows you not to become pigeon-holed and inflexible. It is an opportunity to make more work-related friendships, alliances, and peers. Starting over does not mean a complete severing of old ties, nor does it mean that you discount the past. What makes transitions successful is the ability to take the best of the past and mesh it with the offerings of the present.

People that successfully transition into a new start heal from old wounds and do not let bitterness, anger, disappointment or false perceptions keep them in locked into the past. An example of this is someone who spends a year out of work because they are waiting for the exact same job, they lost at the exact same pay rate. So, they have spent a year not making any money and further accumulating debt because pride and stubbornness refuse to let go of the past "wonderful days." They ignore that when they made the $100,000 a year, they spent $120,000 and did not save or reap the full benefits of the salary.

Now they refuse to take a $70,000 job, which if they budget, and save can, in the end, result in a comfortable lifestyle. When you do not get stuck over the money you used to make, you can work on moving forward and getting back to that salary again from a different job or a different route such as entrepreneurship.

Questions to explore:
*What excites you about learning something new?*
*When was the last time you set bold goals for yourself and stepped out of your comfort zone?*
*Do you see yourself growing or challenging in your position 5 years from now?*

# Struggling with Confusion and Comparison

*People think I am a Bitch!* There is this stereotypical view that strong women are aggressive and was used to accuse women of being masculine in their approach to work. When in reality they are assertive and making sure to have a voice at the decision-making table. They are often admired and celebrated until they become your competition or your boss, then the rules seem to change.

A strong woman is judged harsher and watched in case she makes any wrong moves. Celebrated by some and envied by others. Some co-workers are asking you to mentor and teach them, while you deal with isolation, nitpicking, and backstabbing by some of those same people.

How do you win? How do you get out of the game and focus on managing employees and doing your job? You do exactly that, do your job well and keep it strictly business. The goal is when someone complains about you for it to be laced with facts and if your work was scrutinized that is could stand up in court of law. You work will reveal your talent and abilities. Let other people talk, lie or conceive plans. The truth will win out, don't rush to defend time and truth is on your side.

*Escaping the temptation of comparison*
   *1) Remember the sacrifices you made to get here.*

When someone is envious of you, he or she often has no idea of the price you pay to do what you do. They cannot see or comprehend the personal sacrifices you have given to be where you are or go where you are going. They only see the glory and not the gory part of building what you have. The fatigue, fear, humiliation, fight, and the compromises or conflicts, all go hidden to do what you do. Yet those who are fighting to get in your shoes would not know how to walk in them even it is was given to them.

   *2) Don't waste your energy focused on the wrong things*

Let them wear themselves out trying to outdo you, trying to win or be better, they will eventually unravel themselves. You want to get to a place of confidence where you can say in your heart that "what God has for me is for me and no man or woman can take it or change it."

This is not about promoting a false sense that you are irreplaceable, because no one is irreplaceable. Yet no one can be duplicated, your talents, gifts, and personality are a package deal and unique only to you. Therefore, you are irreplaceable in this respect.

The image of being aggressive is one that is made based on other people's perceptions, beliefs and insecurities. There is little you can do in any of those areas that will change others. Yet there is much that you can do to change how you feel and think about yourself in these areas from now on.

*3) Consistently work on your goals and moving forward*

This is how you avoid the temptation to compare. One thing you can do that will help is consistently be yourself. The more you are truthful and comfortable being authentic, the less you will compare yourself to others. We judge ourselves by unrealistic standards and compare to false stereotypes. No one is perfect or has all the answers, no human being is great at everything and flawless is a goal in things not people.

Focsu on buliding and expressing your true character. It is the least stressful version of you to be in alignment with your values, beliefs and moving towards your goals. We fall out of alignment when we are trying to live someone else's life. Live upright and with integrity with yourself and others, that is balance. It will not always be easy, but it is freedom.

Questions to explore:
*When was the last time you felt misunderstood?*
*How do you build trust and loyalty with people you work with and for?*

## Struggling to Stay Your Lane, Your Gifting

When my kids were younger, it was a humorous sight to see my 2-year-old attempt to exert authority over my 11-year-old. She will try to stand tall and in all her might she will shout her wishes and will on to my 11-year-old, who will in return let out a great big laugh and proceed to ignore her. When my 2-year-old continued with even more insistence, her sister at best tries to appease or distract her with food. It is cute when a toddler tries to be more than their age or wisdom allows for. It is embarrassing, insulting and can be damaging when an adult or someone in leadership steps into a role that they are not equipped for.

I may deeply desire to be a firefighter with all my heart; I may have been told that I will be a great firefighter someday. Yet if I go and put on a firefighter outfit and walk into a fire to rescue someone, without prior training I will risk killing myself and the person I am attempting to save. When we take on a role or position because our ego thinks we can, yet we have no training, experience or mentoring we are deficient. Our showing up amounts to being like the emperor with no clothes on who thinks he is dressed in the finest apparel.

There is great peace, contentment, and success when we operate at the level of our gifting and strengths. When we stop trying to take on more than we are equipped or ready to handle, we allow others the opportunity for others to get in their rightful places. If we are in an orchestra and I a violinist find myself sitting in the chair of the clarinet player then as a whole, we will find ourselves missing a sound and out of tune because I am taking a seat that belongs to someone else.

We must stay in our level of gifting, which is our level of power, authority, and influence. Our level and place are where we will find great success and is where our gifts will find nurturing and training. Someone else's level of gifting or place will bring us stress, restlessness, and great anxiety because we cannot keep up with it or succeed at that which we were not created for.

God is not obligated to help you succeed in what He has not created for your life. If it is not God's will for your life, then you will struggle to prosper in that thing. Whether it is a relationship, a job, a hobby or a specific area of interest, if it distracts you from your destiny, then you will not prosper in it. The longer we remain in someone else's lane, chair or place of gifting the longer we are away from our own.

## Questions to explore:

*Which role or position have you had the most success?*
*What has past failures taught you?*
*What comes naturally to you to perform?*
*When have others called you a natural or talented?*

## **Struggling to Live Courageously**

Have you ever examined people who have accomplished extraordinary things in the face of adversity and thought to yourself how did they do? Were they fearful or did it come naturally? My experience has been that anything that I have ever accomplished that was noteworthy or extraordinary came after I faced at times extraordinary fear.

Fear is that emotion and enemy that is common and will come to paralyze you when you attempt to do anything great, life-changing, or character developing. We want to naturally avoid anything that is uncomfortable and may result in embarrassment. We will reason it, we will shirk it off, but there will come a time where you will have to say and do the hard stuff. You may have to share something with a loved one that will hurt their feelings and may bring tension into the relationship, yet it will have to be said.

Every relationship will be tested, yet if it emerges from that testing intact and respected, then it will grow healthy. There will come a time in your life where you do not have the time or energy for many relationships. Therefore you will have to pick and choose wisely which relationships you invest in and nurture.

For some, they are quicker to give up a relationship than to work through the hard stuff. The hard stuff may involve the other person being angry at you, or to listen to how you may have disappointed them. The hard stuff will mean conveying to them what you do not agree with and looking in the mirror of their eyes to see your faults and shortcomings. Any relationship that you have deemed worth investing in will have a time where you must face conflict in it.

It is a natural first reaction to being disappointed or having someone betray your trust is to shut down on sharing and raise up the wall of protection. Not all disagreements, miscommunication or failures mean the end of a relationship. Some relationships are worth a second try, forgiveness and deeper experience in trust.

The conflict will prove the relationship for what it is, either it will grow and become stronger, or it will weaken and fade away. If it proves to not have a strong foundation or thread of love running through it, then it may end offense. Your challenge will be to first decide how important this relationship is to you. If it is important and a God-orchestrated relationship do you best to make peace, compromise so that all parties win and feel valued and mend the wounds. If the relationship is not God ordained, do your best to end the relationship with peace and extending much grace.

## Questions to explore:

*Are you willing to trust again if it meant you would have the kind of friendship you always wanted?*

*Who would you pursue a relationship with if you were not afraid?*

*What has afraid kept you from accomplishing with others?*

## Struggling When It's Time to Move On

If you are feeling the winds of change coming, if there are hints in the air, financial tight spots, movement of people into different positions, sudden changes in policy and things that do not seem to add up as they are being sold. These are signs that can keep you from making the mistake of believing lies that will get you stuck. Being a little suspicious or cautious in the corporate world helps keep you sharp.

Some people believe the lie "I'm irreplaceable," because of their talents, their connections or the amount of revenue they have brought into the company. No one is irreplaceable and when your ego tempts you to believe this tell yourself that there is someone coming up behind you younger, stronger hungrier, and willing to do what it takes to get your job. Keep this in mind that some of those friendships may only last while you are employed, and some of the loyalties will last as long as you are fresh, and the talk of the day.

*When you are trying to discern if it is time to move on consider the following:*

As the company changes hands before leaving take every opportunity to introduce yourself (personality, skills, abilities) to the new management. When doing so use situations as they present themselves to demonstrate what you are capable of. After doing this give it time to evaluate how your skills are received. Look for clues, where you fit within this new merger and the opportunities for growth then give it a chance. Assign a deadline to see if the outcome and opportunities are favorable to your goals. With any new merger or change in the way of doing business you have to let the dust settle and the rumors subside before making hasty decisions.

*Some signs that it may be time to move on are:*

<u>Job stress</u> - the job can become stressful for many reasons, such as not enough qualified employees for the duties available, increasing tensions due to politics, a management structure that is oppressive or out of touch with employees, work has overtaken personal life, feeling underappreciated and overworked.

<u>Outgrown the job</u> - there will come a time where you have mastered the work, you find yourself doing in three hours what took eight hours before. Then you are left with time to goof off, pursue other interest or just simply avoid management. The monotony of the work has crept in the same people are doing the same stupid things, and meetings have become a predictable song and dance.

You have more experience and talents under your belt that you have not been able to properly utilize at the job.

<u>You dread going to work</u> – Monday morning has come too soon, and Friday is too far off. When you get in the car, you dread getting out the car, you're tired and when you enter the building your attitude instantly changes. If you hear one more complaint, you feel like you are going to explode. Your family hears nothing, but complaints and your co-workers get nothing but attitude. You are left feeling bad, tired and restless; these are the signs it's time to change your perspective, attitude or move on.

<u>Boredom starting to creep into your routine</u>- asking the question when is this going to becoming challenging? Boredom can steal from your employer and rob you of your enthusiasm. When we are bored, this can lead to making poor decisions and get involved in projects and situations that are not necessarily beneficial.

Strong women keep their eyes open and ear attentive to opportunity. When you have tested and examined your status at work, then you can make decisions about your future.

<u>Questions to explore:</u>
*When did you stop enjoying the work, what happened?*

*What are the thoughts and feelings you have when thinking about work?*

*How can you change these thoughts into productive, motivating thoughts to help propel you forward?*

*How can you leave in a positive way, creating opportunities for the future?*

## Struggling to Not Follow, The Herd

In business employees are urged to strive for visible positions; the problem with being in very visible positions is that you win big and fail big. When you are being offered a noticeable position in the company, be careful to examine the position before accepting what may look like a great prospect yet it can be a dead end for your career. This can be a position with limited opportunity to develop, and if you are trying to make a move-out or up, it is obvious.

Your visibility at work can be a trap in a position that you cannot get out of unless you leave the company. Your company could be using you in this visible position to look diverse and progressive, yet you need to use it to get in publications and media to benefit your career goals. Before accepting the position determine whether your success and results can be quantified and attributed to you while in the position. Test this by developing a resume with your current position can you prove your value; can you prove your contributions.

Avoid the position if it looks like it will go nowhere, do not fall victim to your visibility. If you accept the position without being strategic, you may find that it fails to live up to expectation. If you accept the position successfully exploit that visibility to rise through the ranks or obtain financial reward.

Craft a plan for your career progression within the company before one is crafted for you. This will take courage, planning, actively seeking clarity, understanding, and truth about yourself. You are a strong woman, and it is not worth your time to take on a project that does not agree with your principles. You are too smart, too creative to follow the thinking of the masses, define your stance, express your perspective and lead the pack to innovation.

Understand the relationship of your position to the company's overall objectives. Be wise and purposeful in your decisions and business relationships to make every action and interaction profitable to you. Taking a risk does not mean taking on a project that is big, has not been researched, lacking clearly defined objectives. To avoid foolish mistakes take your time making decisions, be clear as to the purpose and expected the end of any project or position. Let nothing take you by surprise when it is possible to know beforehand.

Remember just because everyone is saying the same thing does not mean they are correct. Test everything against your gut, the facts and investigate upcoming trends to not get left behind. Don't be afraid of being different or the first to embrace a new way of thinking, companies invest in #1 and follow the leading of those who deliver success. Set yourself apart from the crowd; let your name be associated with innovation, results, confidence, and success.

Questions to explore:
*How would you do things differently at the job if given a chance to improve where you are?*
*What makes you unique in your position?*
*What is the impact you are having?*
*How can you make an even bigger impact?*

## Struggling with Opportunities and Risk

Opportunities are made through volunteering for task and projects that others shy away from. This does not mean to take on assignments that may lead to dead ends, but take ones on that you can produce tangible, noticeable results. When something is being offered investigate, weigh the pros and cons, do not be afraid that you will lose out if you do not say yes right away. You will find with committees or projects that the people who may have initiated it or begun with the project are not always the ones that complete it. There are often opportunities to join later when someone must resign from the project or does not have the skills to get the job done. Give yourself the opportunity to learn and investigate before committing to anything. You do not want to be stuck with an elephant size dead-end project if you are trying to make career moves.

Opportunities can also be found through problem-solving. Fixing dilemmas saving the company money or saving a sale, recovering a client. Problem solvers are viewed as creative, intelligent and someone you want on your team. They bring energy, enthusiasm and help others to feel empowered especially when the team is in unfamiliar territory. You may not have the answers but having the confidence and wit to find the answer is the next best thing. To a project manager, it is like having money in the bank; you feel secure going forward.

You can make opportunities by offering new ideas, creative ways to increase business, better serve customers, and save the company money. Opportunity often presents itself during the downturn of business. You can brainstorm ways to increase sales in a month where sales are traditionally down. This is creating what does not exist and taking a risk believing that it can work and cause you to shine as a result.

Opportunities are also found by being entrepreneurial in your thinking. Businesses are looking for ways to become much more efficient and are focused on long-term sustainability. Entrepreneurial thinking in your career can help you become even more valuable to the company with innovations and ideas that can lead to greater success.

For the entrepreneur who is not ready to take the leap yet, you can use this time wisely by saving money to invest in your dream later. There is a quote that says success is preparation meeting opportunity. Saving money now to invest in your business later is just one step you can take in getting yourself ready for future success. Success is waiting down the road for all those willing to invest, plan, prepare the ground and then till the ground. Your future business is the ground that can bring you a great harvest if you invest in it now.

One of the benefits of working a steady job is a steady income. Use some of it and save a portion every time you get paid towards your future business or next career move. This is a great way to see your exit strategy beginning to take shape. Keep this money separate and make it hard to access so that you are not tempted to save and spend. By saving money to invest in your dream, you are sending a strong message to your heart that business ownership is possible and to your mind that you are serious about this endeavor. Start today, and you will be on your way to business ownership and freedom from the 9 to 5 rat race.

Taking risk does not mean saying yes to everything out of obligation, competition or because your mentor suggested it. There will come a time you have to make your own decisions and do what is best for your career and what you feel competent and capable of succeeding at. That choice is not always given, but when it chooses wisely.

Questions to explore:
*How has your past success stifled or stopped your growth?*
*Where do you see opportunities to provide, create change?*
*How can you be the solution to the problem in front of you?*

## Struggling to Use Time Effectively

When you find yourself saying "if I had more time, more help, more money" Stop! This is the beginning of excuses that make the very thing we desire to do, not get done. When you wait for the perfect timing and circumstances to do all the things you have been putting off it may never come. Life is never perfect, although there are times when everything lines up just enough to enable you to complete a goal. For example, having an appointment get canceled that frees up your time to accomplish a task or errand, you may have put off. The opportunity can come in bigger forms such as your children going to school fulltime freeing your daytime hours to go to school yourself or find part-time employment to earn extra cash. Strong women avoid regret statements, which can rend you unproductive.

Have you ever said, I can't wait to do ___" speaking of an opportunity to accomplish something that is important? Yet, when the moment arrives you use time unwisely and find yourself sleeping, entertaining, doing busy work until nothing productive or intentional gets accomplished. We fill our precious time with the unnecessary task, which are often unrelated to what was originally intended. When the opportunity comes to check off a major item on your to-do list use it and do the very thing you have been waiting to do. You can be free from the regret that comes with "would of, could of, should of" statements. Just do the very thing that you feel pressed to do. Accomplish it today, little by little and do it intentionally.

Use your time more effectively by limiting time with the friends who cause the kind of distractions that are fun or feel helpful, but after a full day you are left accomplishing nothing you set out to do. Having fun is important because being driven and successful you probably tend to work and never relax, yet when you are in a season of transition, your time becomes more valuable, and you have to plan and use it wisely.

Use your time effectively now to get the results you are looking. Discipline yourself to see your goals achieved. Do not lose focus or give yourself away to others and wind up leaving your goals unaccomplished.

Strong women stay on task; multitasking will slow you down in achieving results. It is not effective if your goal is quality, not quantity. If you are exhausted with having too many things on your to-do list and never checking off more than 2-3, then stop the multitasking and start focusing. You may find that you are more effective giving set amount of time to each task and sticking to it, till it is complete. I have found that there is an emotional reward attached to completing the task and not seeing them again on your list. As you see results this helps fuel a desire to get more results; starting a pattern of completed projects and task. Patterns of positive results will feed your spirit with encouragement and motivation.

Focusing on one thing at a time helps to ensure the task is done right. As a strong woman you cannot afford to produce work that is sloppy or second rate, therefore focus on guaranteeing better work. To help you even further in learning to focus, resist the temptation to give in to distractions. For example, when working on project avoid answering the text or phone until a set time to follow up. Focus, and you will finish whatever you have set out to do.

Questions to explore:
*What are the time stealers in your life?*
*How can you protect your time?*
*Are your values matching up with how you invest your time?*
*What are the things, commitments or activities you can reduce or eliminate to make more time?*

## Struggling with When and How to Listen

Listening and taking in information with all your senses is one of the most powerful ways to communicate and connect with others. In business and in life the power of being able to communicate with another in a way that produces the desired result is a great ability. From the people you work with to those you meet in the course of doing business everyone has a need to be listened to, understood and respected. If you are trying to win over others, sell something or leave a lasting impression. Not only is the act of listening important but handling what has been said with care by understanding and applying the knowledge correctly.

For some keeping our mouths shut becomes difficult because we are afraid, we will not be heard, understood or make the impression we are seeking. We think ourselves more important than we should. Therefore, we speak to be heard not to be understood or connect. In an age where people are using all types of gadgets to communicate more frequently from anywhere and anytime, we are understanding and having real dialogue-less and less. We need to listen because it is how we gather information, stay on top and in the know of what's happening around us. There is a danger in not seeing what is up ahead because we are become subject to the changes and may be left unable to navigate.

Communicating successfully will help you make friends, discern what your enemies are up to. It will help you serve others by meeting an expressed need. If your boss is having trouble solving a personal problem such as daycare for their child and you know of a daycare resource your attention to this personal need can help you win them over as a friend. You hear a coworker has a parent that is sick, a card or word of encouragement can go a long way to win points with that co-worker. Giving someone who is having a bad day the opportunity to get a break with some privacy may be a favor that comes back to you when you need some space.

Your family and friends need you to master listening, to deepen your relationship and interactions with them. If you have ever heard these phrases from your family or friends, it's a sign there is broken communication.

If you hear:

*"you're not listening"*

*"you're not getting anything I'm saying to you"*

*"Stop trying to fix it and listen"*

*"I am not one of your clients"*

*"I don't work for you don't talk to me like that"*

These are statements that reveal if your listening and understanding skills need help. Your friends and loved ones are saying something is happening when they talk to make them feel like you are not connecting or understanding them. The next time you hear any one of these phrases ask the next question, what am I doing or saying to make you feel not heard or understood. Improving how you listen, understand, take time to show compassion, be present and engaged can help in the struggles or the stress in the relationship.

Questions to explore:
*When was the last time you listened without interrupting and was fully present mind and body?*
*How can you improve your communication and listening skills?*
*What are the corrections or complains your friends have made about communicating with you?*

## Struggling with Lack of Clarity

Some people will say I don't know if I have a dream? For those who say "I do not know if I have a dream," you want to look at what is blocking you from your dream. Sometimes the cares of life, our obligations, commitments and the busyness of life block us from seeing our dream clearly. When we are too busy doing for others or living a life that is not really what we want, the dream will dim or seem nonexistent.

Everyone who is living, and breathing has a dream; the difference is that some are living that dream and others have it buried. If you are not living your dream chances are it is buried under questions, doubts, and cares of life. Often, we busy ourselves with things we do not enjoy doing and what brings us joy may get 10% of our time. The other issues are doing what you have always wanted to do, yet it lacks enjoyment you find yourself saying is "this all there is?" and not producing results. This is what happens when the dream is not in its right setting.

You may need to change your perspective or just change the way you are doing things. You can be in the right venue yet the wrong arena, and that is as damaging as being in the wrong venue altogether. Let's say for example you want always wanted to be a doctor, yet when you reach your goal, you are a doctor for people or a health company that does not support your area of expertise or shares your values. Here you are right dream and wrong atmosphere.

Is this the limit of what I can do? If you limit your creativity, the answer is yes, if you look beyond what you know and are comfortable with then the answer is no. In this global, technology-driven world your ideas have no limit to what you can do. Complacency is an enemy to greatness avoid complacency make your dream even bigger, do not stop where you are.

The first step in getting clarity is to practice dream as you did when you were young. This time with the goal of identifying and narrow down the thing which makes your heart soar and your passion come alive. Dreaming is one exercise I enjoy escaping the realities of this present life to a canvas that is without limit and where I feel in control of the outcome. Since I was a kid, I have dreamed of being everything from a school teacher to a fighter pilot. My real life has tried to match my dreams by taking me around the globe helping people, enjoy sights, cultures, and helping bring solutions to larger issues. Dreams are what keep people happy and hopeful when life presented situations that were difficult.

Dreams can give you direction as you move forward in life. There are dreams of you conquering the world that you had in abundance as a child, yet are rare in adulthood as the realities of life set in. The dreams that were wonderful and grand until we share them with the dream killers, those whose canvas of dreams have been defiled or determined by others.

As you begin to share your dreams with true believers and supporter's one thing will be evident in speaking there will be a childlike wonderment in your eyes. There will be joy and uncertainty in your voice. Yet what will surprise you is the intimate, exciting and being fully awake moment that will occur. God gives us a dream of becoming or doing something like a glimpse into our future and as a gentle and tangible reminder of the scripture that says all things are possible.

Questions to explore:
*If you list everything, you currently do and subtract all the things you don't enjoy what is left?*
*If fear and doubt were gone what would you dare to do?*
*Who do you admire and what about them do you want to imitate?*
*What is something you do that makes you feel alive, free and living out the truth of who you are?*

# Struggling to Win with the Hand You're Dealt

T.D. Jakes Founder of The Potters House said that "you can win with the hand you were dealt." This made me think about how we often talk about life dealing us a bad hand. How do some win with a bad hand and others seem to fold under the hand?

Let's take some lessons from an old country song by Kenny Rogers. The song says "you've got to know when to hold" "know when to fold em"; "know when to walk away"; "know when to run." You can find some truth in the songs we sing. Learning how to work with what you are given, learning how to play your hand can be the difference of a life lived successfully despite great opposition. Some people face life with impossible odds yet become resilient and use the figurative mud thrown on them to build stepping stones out of difficult places and others faced the same challenges yet give in to a mediocre and under constant turmoil.

How you see yourself, and the situation will determine the choices you make. The choices you make become the building blocks for your future. These will one day be looked back upon as the pivotal turning point towards success or failure in your life.

"Knowing when to hold em." This can be applied to knowing when to hold back from reacting. Your child can come home one day, and their hair is dyed blue because they wanted to try it, testing the limits of your patience by blaming others for convincing them it was a good idea. In this case, you can you can choose to convey your disapproval while holding back from overreacting turning this into a teaching moment rather than an explosive argument.

When you are being tested by people, you may want to hold back. Although this very thought is against our human nature, it can produce great results. Holding back allows you to get a true sense of what is happening and provides an opportunity to make better decisions. It allows you to choose your words wisely and turn the moment around to produce the results you want.

Questions to explore:
*How can you make the best of a bad situation?*
*What are the lessons to learn in this situation to prepare for the future?*
*When have you waited in the past and things worked out for good or the issue resolved on its own?*

## **Struggling with Feeling Unsatisfied**

When you first imagined the career and all the benefits that followed you said, "I will be happy when, I get that title, office, that position". Now you are in the position and still unhappy. The salary is great and more than most people in the United States make in year, but it does not feel like it's enough. You are starting to question why your stuff, the car, house, title and memberships are not giving you the contentment or happiness you thought it would have.

You are working more hours than ever, and when you get the vacation you too tired to enjoy it. The accumulation of stuff now has you hiring other people to manage the stuff, services to protect the stuff and taking your energy to think about the stuff. The family seems to enjoy the benefits until they remind you, they want more, the next big release, newer shinier version of the phone, laptop or car.

This leaves you asking them and yourself when is enough, what number of things, what version will be satisfying so you don't have to work as hard forever. You think to yourself, I don't know any more what will make me happy, I just know this is not it.

To win in this area begins with separating your sense of worth or value from the things in your life. Things can become status symbols if we let it, but what if you shifted your mindset to see the stuff as memories, moments and toys for pleasure not status. The stuff has price tags that are determined by the makers without much reasoning other than what you and the market are willing to pay for it.

To examine your relationship with your stuff, lets explore the following questions:

- Can I sustain this lifestyle in retirement?
- Is the lifestyle I created making me happy?
- What from the past am I trying to erase, make up for or fix with the present?
- Who did I learn my spending habits from?
- How would life be easier or simpler if I let go of some of the stuff?
- Do I invest more in things or people?
- Is my investment for the future, retirement and legacy as much as I invest in the things and the present pleasure?
- With each salary increase am I spending more, less or the same and why?
- Am I spending on what I care about the most?
- What would it take to know I made it and reached my goals?
- What am I really chasing after with each accomplishment?
- How will I know when I reach it?

These questions are designed to help you uncover and start to separate the link between things and feelings of happiness. The things are the ability to make you happy are short term. Measuring your satisfaction is long term, satisfaction has to do with contentment, peace and gratitude about what you have. Dissatisfaction is tied to what you don't have, what you are not doing, missing the mark of perfection.

Satisfaction is when you are full, not missing or lacking anything. The gratefulness of a good day, a smile, hug, appreciation from your loved ones. Its when what you need is met with what you have. I needed to feel loved today and then you got an "I love you" from your partner. You needed to feel appreciated and your co-workers said thank you for your help on a project. You need the right mixer to make a cake and you had the mixer at home or found a way to mix and complete the cake without the perfect equipment.

Having things are vehicles to happiness not sources of it, its can be a tool to experience moments of joy, contentment and place for the building of memories. This is just one way of no longer measuring your happiness or satisfaction by the number of things owned or acquired.

# Round Three
# Spiritual Life

If you are tempted to skip over this round, don't do it. If you neglect the spiritual side of you, then you are neglecting a powerful source of life, everlasting love, and true freedom. We are spirit beings in a world that often wants us to live out only a portion of who we are and when we come up short, feeling like something is missing, we are left without answers.

Give God a chance to take over the burdens you carry. To help you understand and process and overcome the pain; to make life sweeter and to go beyond happiness to real and lasting joy. Let's stay in the ring and explore the part of the battle where you don't fight alone and yes, you win.

Let's get this fight started right now! The battle between the real "me" and "the me" I hope to become. There is a blow by blow fight going on daily in our head; we fight the messages of the past, the reality of the present and hope of the future, all with the words that we allow to come in our mind and flow out our lips. Words that are punching and bruising our self-esteem daily.

We take a slap to our self-confidence when we look in the mirror and focus on everything that is wrong about us. We take knock out blows to our self-assurance when making mistakes, fail at something or get devastating news that challenges our sense of security. How we perceive ourselves influences our level of success, joy, and contentment.

## Struggling to Celebrate Solo

You have come to a place where you will have to walk alone. There are times in life learning to be alone is gift, because in that time you can get to know yourself deeper. There are also practical situations which others will not be able to go with you are be present to support you but are behind you 100% in your goal or in celebrating your achievement.

The feeling of loneliness is a different factor, this is when you feel a loss or abandoned because someone who should provide physically, or emotional support is not available, and the sense of abandonment or loss is growing inside your heart.

Feeling alone is a temporary emotion that will go away once the event or moment in time passes and something happens to remind you that you are not alone permanently. The feeling of loneliness takes a lot more time, unpacking the emotions and challenging of the thoughts to overcome.

The spiritual key to combating loneliness is confidence that God has not left you although people will. To know that God's purpose for your life will be realized and that it is not people that bring it about nor people that stop it.

The mental key is to begin with being honest about your thoughts they might sound like "I don't need them anyway," or "they would just bring me down." When you are thinking about who should have been there to support you in your big moment. Reasoning to yourself will provide momentary relief, but it will solve the long-term problem. Instead look at the thoughts, feelings and behaviors that are keeping you isolated and feeling lonely.

Let's try this example, you invited your sister to two of your events in the past and one event she did show up or call and the second event she was embarrassingly late and walked in during your acceptance speech and you stopped inviting to future events. Below is a chart demonstrating how the thoughts and decisions can lead to unhealthy or healthy outcomes.

| Unhealthy | Healthy |
|---|---|
| The thought: "no cares about anything I do, and no one will ever support me" | The thought: "my family cares, some of them are more reliable with time and commitments than others" |
| The feeling: "unloved and lonely" | The feeling: "loved, connected" |
| The behavior: "I not going to invite them to anything, or tell | The behavior: "I have to plan ahead and invite to the right people to the |

| them when something special is happening, so I'm not disappointed" | right event or give the late ones a 1-hour early arrival time" |
|---|---|
| The result: "I don't invite any friends or family, and no one is there to support me" | The result: "there is someone in my corner at the special events who I don't have to worry about" |

Beverly thought to herself while waiting for her award. *"All the people shaking my hand and saying, this is amazing, incredible, you should be so proud, I would do anything to have your life. I find myself thinking, without someone to share to success, and accomplishments with is does not feel special. I have won many awards and have been to several recognition ceremonies alone. It is ironic to have a room full of people celebrating or admiring your achievements, but I would gladly give it up to have someone special share with."*

How do you keep your head up when being asked "who's here with you" and you have to say no one? Do you make excuses for them? Do you start to recite your woes? Do you despise the achievement you have made because no one close seems to care?

You do none of the above, your achievements are still valid even if no one special to you knows about them. Your course is set, and often God is the one promoting you and giving the gift of success, and He wants you to enjoy it. Enjoy it because the giver of the gift deserves respect and recognition; enjoy it because it is a testimony to your ability, focus, determination and willingness to press forth during adversity, uncertainty and sometimes great fear. You may be robbed once because you are alone in your walk towards success, but you would be committing a double robbery if you did not "celebrate you" where you are at. Refusing to hold your head up high is giving in to the true enemy in your mind, not just the people who did not believe or were negative and nonsupportive. If you do not hold your head up and believe in yourself then who will.

Celebrating solo is a gift to you, never miss the opportunity to be proud of what you have accomplished and look forward to continued success. This act of celebration, acknowledgment, and honor gives life and affirmations to your future goals. Walking alone is never easy but determine in your heart to walk with your head held high, determined, joyful and generous spirit.

Questions to explore:
*What are the things you enjoy doing alone?*
*How can you practice being kind to yourself?*
*When was the last time you celebrated yourself just because of something you enjoyed or was proud of?*

## Struggling to Get Up From The Hospital Bed

When I gave birth to twins, I had to have surgery they call cesarean because both babies were breached. Meaning they were standing up in the womb instead for upside down facing the exit point. Well, I had no real understanding that this was major surgery until they began to prepare me for it and then wheel me into the operating room.

I think they tell you as little as possible to avoid fear, yet the lack of knowledge causes you to be unprepared for the recovery which will take considerably more time than you expected. For me after the surgery in which you are cut open, your major organs moved aside and out then later placed in, pushed down and you're sown or stapled back together. Then you are wheeled away, given painkillers and told to get up and walk it's for your own good. Well, I found myself hunched over, barely able to walk, cold, dizzy, nausea and in pain.

The three days to recover went by too fast, most of the time I was in extreme pain and forced to learn and produce basic body functions under pain and pressure. Then I am told well you have to go home, barely able to walk, hold myself up or go to the bathroom. I am thinking all awhile noooooo I'm not ready yet." "I need more time" "this is not fair." I am crying to my husband I do not know how I am going to make it and I am overwhelmed. Dizzy, coming down and off heavy pain meds, in pain and facing me outside the hospital doors was 3 kids, two school age and a toddler and now newborn twins. Also, my husband who was in the military at the time was only up for the birth and had to return to his assignment right after I got out of the hospital. I thought there was no way.

    I share this in detail with you to show we can survive and succeed after we have been through major events in our lives even though we may feel unprepared. I felt unprepared and unable to make it outside of the hospital even with help and a backup plan in case something goes wrong. You can make it, more time on the hospital bed does not mean that you will get better. In some cases, we become reliant and comfortable in the artificial environment and will not allow ourselves to stretch and adapt after the change or the surgery has taken place.

    When something is changed, removed or repaired in our lives, we must allow time to adjust, time to relearn or learn. We must allow the stretch of our faith muscles to work by moving forward. When we have a clean bill of health and the doctor, says to move forward then we must or run the risk of muscle atrophy or suffering emotionally right where we are stuck.

The ability to rebound from disappointment, setback or a sudden change may come easily in one area of your life and prove difficult in another area.

Questions to explore:
*What change has taken place that you are finding difficult to adjust or rebound from?*
*What steps are you willing to take to heal from the illness or injury?*
*How has illness or injury changed your perspective?*

## Struggling to Feel Valued and Validated

My daughters when they were small came jubilantly and anxiously around report card time to show me their grades. These report cards demonstrated the hard work they put into their school work in the months prior. I look on reviewing each line and class carefully looking not, for perfection but a demonstration that they did their very best with their gifts and talents. When we see the results, they get a great big well done and possible cash or food incentive tied to that, validating their effort, their intelligence, and commitment. I appreciate them and show that I believe in them, and their ability to accomplish their goals.

In the months preceding their report card and every day I value them by supporting them in the daily work that they do in school and at home in an effort to achieve their goals. Our heavenly father is the same way. He validates and values us; His great and perfect creation. Even if what we do is not perfect, we were made in the image of perfection, and we came with nothing missing. This is not to say that we are without sin, the perfection I speak of is that God had a plan for us and he created us perfectly with that plan.

Therefore, the one who created us says He values us by giving His best, by caring for us, by guiding and keeping us.

This is regardless of where we are in a relationship with Him. God's value of us is placed by Him. Therefore we are precious in His sight, and His love for us cannot be measured. God validates us in through His plan for our lives. He causes us to follow that plan and all along the way He is there saying "go for it", " you can do it", " nothing is impossible for those who believe", " I am with you", "success is in your hand" " I love you", "fear not", "trust me" and "good job".

God validates your worth and your experiences in life by using them for His purposes. Helping you to discover something of value from your ashes and tears, God redeems your life and your times, causing good to rise out of bad.

Questions to explore:
*Do you remember a time when you felt validated and why?*
*What or who made you question your value?*
*What would it take to know you are valued?*
*What are the ways you can challenge the negative thoughts about yourself?*

## Struggling to Know Their Worth

How do I know that I valuable to God? This was a hard concept for me to swallow. God loving me, the "me" that I know was at one time full of anger and bitterness. The girl that once wanted to make those who had hurt me hurt just as bad. This person had a hard time believing and accepting God's love because I wanted to know why, I went through the physical and sexual abuse. I wanted to know where God was when I was hurt and neglected. I wanted to know why He just did not prevent it all or make the people responsible pay.

In order to believe that I was valuable to God, He had to change my perspective and remove the wall of fear and love me out of the pain. I expected God to be distant, all knowing and all punishing. I thought that God only cared that I was a sinner and just wanted to point out all my flaws, mistakes and sins. But it was not until I began to pursue a real relationship with God that I learned about God wanting to show me His love for me, not condemnation.

I slowly learned my perception of God was shaped by my environment and upbringing. My environment taught me that God was distant; my upbringing taught me that He was harsh. People often spoke as God the father, and I knew that my father not only denied me for many years but was distant and our relationship was awkward when I did find him. Yet that was not the true character of God; I began to meet people who really knew what a relationship with God meant.

I met all types of people over the years with various degrees and expressions of their relationship with God. The one person who was kind to me and seemed to know a gentle, caring side of God, while struggling with addiction whose church services was conducted through the television by the television preacher, and although she never went to church, she always encouraged me to go. I met real people who loved God and battled in one area or another, but their love for God and relationship with God was genuine although it had flaws. They were unassuming, loving and generous in love. I learned from them that if God could love and meet them in struggle, He could love and meet me where I was; not to leave me in that state but to take me higher and give my life purpose, direction, and abundance.

So how did I learn that I was valuable to God? All the years I was struggling to survive a harsh childhood, lonely teenage years and the ups and downs of transitioning to adulthood God was there. God showed me love through the people he sent in my life; he showed me kindness and another side of human beings through people that loved him and had a life and spiritual practice that incorporated God. They were not perfect people, but they knew a perfect God. I saw ordinary people in struggle and yet continue to love and thank God.

There was a desire growing inside of me that I did not comprehend, it was a desire to have their joy, a desire to know God as they knew him, to selfishly at first get answers to my many questions. Later it became a desire to just find peace, because, after all my achievements, I was still not content nor had any peace of mind or heart; I was struggling in my private life to live a life that was on the outside well put together, a woman liked by everyone, fun to be with and driven to be successful. Yet when night came or when I was all alone, I struggled with the nightmares of the past, insecurity, loneliness, and fear.

God showed me I was valuable to him by preserving my life in some very dangerous situations that I found myself in. He ensured that my teen years were spent in a place where I could begin to explore who I am and what my talents and gifts were. Although my teen years were spent living in a group home for young girls, I ended up in an agency that was able to provide for my physical needs. God sent people into my life that were like angels to me serving as mentors and mother figures while my natural mother was not able too.

God showed me I was valuable through the many opportunities he opened for me. It was God operating in a very tangible way in my life that helped me to see how valuable I was to Him.

Questions to explore:
*Who has made you feel special in the past?*
*What happened in your past to make you feel not worthy?*
*How would you describe God's presence in your life?*
*Who are the people in your life that have shown you, love?*

## Struggling with Loneliness

What do you do when you feel lonely, abandoned, forgotten? There are times when we can get busy doing things; doing things for others, doing something that will help us move forward in life. Those are helpful ways to take your mind off your loneliness' or your pain. There will come a time where you will not have anything more to occupy your time, and you will find yourself forced to deal with the loneliness. That is a scary and painful time for anyone who has had to face their loneliness. You may find yourself trying to come up with solutions, trying to cling on to others who make you feel less lonely, trying to hurry up and solve the issue.

The loneliness can seem so unbearable that you may find yourself willing to compromise just to make the sting of loneliness go away. Compromising by saying you are sorry even if it just continues to perpetuate the problem; by living with someone who is abusing you; by burying your desires and allowing someone else to continue in their selfishness. Compromising by lowering standards just to be accepted; selling yourself short, by giving away something you treasure in exchange for something temporary affection. Compromising to have a warm body in the bed next to you, despite that they belong to someone else's.

Why is being alone with ourselves and God so difficult? Why is it that we must be surrounded by constant noise, activity, and drama? Why is it that we pay for vacations where we don't rest? Complain of needing "me time" and alone time and yet constantly fill up our schedules. Why is it that we equate the silence with bad and we confuse busyness with productivity? Why do we fear to learn about ourselves as we really are?

Finding the answers for all of these will help your discover areas that need your attention, fears that have been masked and the key to finding a greater peace in your life. There are many reasons being alone can be frightening and perceived as something to avoid.

*A few reasons we avoid the silence:*
* You fear to find out that you are not who you have been portraying to others.
* You might learn that something has to change in your life.
* You may have to begin healing or bringing closure to something in your life.
* You may find out that your life up until now has been mundane.

* You may discover there are more questions than answers.
* You may have to make sense of all your chaos in your life.
* You may have to deal with the thinking or other issues that is causing you to feel lonely.

There are many other reasons we avoid being truly alone, yet when it catches up to us, and there is nowhere else to run and nothing else to do we have to find ourselves turning to God. God is the way to peace, comfort and inner strength. His Spirit can help you not to compromise or manipulate when you feel tempted to do so. This is when you remember God. Remember God because He remembers you. Remember God because He is the only who can fill the emptiness you feel when everything is silent.

Remember God by setting your mind on God, by talking with Him and being honest about your fears, hurt and pain. Talk to God and share; confront those issues that have nagged at you for so long. Admit to God where you are, what you feel and what you need. Practice spending time with God, when the loneliness' creeps up on you. Ask God to come where you are at your moment of weakness to give you a way out. When you are feeling strong, continue to remember God, continue to call on him and thank him for everything.

Remember God because He remembers you and when you are weak, He becomes even stronger in your life because you can totally lean on him.

God is trustworthy and able to do what He says, while as a good father, he can be what you need at the moment.

Questions to explore:
*Are you isolating yourself from others and why?*
*Have you been productive in your goals or busy?*
*What are the stumbling blocks on your spiritual road?*
*What are your expectations in a spiritual relationship?*

## Struggling Not Just Make it, be Victorious

If we could go through life seeing ourselves as God see us, life would be easier. We would have more days where we felt on empowered, free and stronger. We would wake up in the morning feeling as if nothing is impossible. If we saw ourselves as God sees us then loving ourselves with all our baggage, faults and flaws would not be a problem. We would likely take better care of our health and slow down and celebrate the quirks in our personality. If we see God as this all-powerful presence then naturally as a child of God, we will inherit some of that power.

The word of God says that "greater is He that is within you than He that is in the world." What does this really mean for us mere humans? It means that if you are connected to God in a relationship, and He resides in your heart by His Holy Spirit, then God inside of you is bigger than anything on the outside of you. God in you is greater than your problems, fears, shortcomings. God in you is greater than your enemies, past hurts, false accusations, and limitations. God in you is bigger than the mountain of obstacles in front of you. If this is all so and God resides in you, then there will not be one fight that you cannot or will not win if you believe this truth.

If the bible which describes God and all His characteristics, abilities and virtues names Jesus as a conquering King, then by right of inheritance and relationship then you are also a conquer. Overcoming and winning every battle and ultimately the war against your destiny just by believing; just by virtue of relationship and inheritance.

The next time you feel the sting of life burning in your heart and pain of your hopes being crushed remember that you have not lost. In a battle, a Solider may get wounded, but the wound does not say that they have been defeated; it simply reveals the intensity of the battle. Your wounds do not declare you as a defeated, yet we tend to think the wound, or the pain is a sign of loss or weakness. Yet the greater the wound, it demonstrates the force and fierceness in which the enemy of your life is coming at you.

Every day you get up and get back in the battle, every day that you choose to believe the best about God and His work in your life; every day that you do not quit or compromise then, you are victorious. Conquering does not always mean taking someone else down and you rising up. Conquering can simply be continuing on when others quit; being a conquer involves defeating those negative thoughts than hold you back. It means going beyond the natural or self-imposed limitations on your life to accomplish something extraordinary.

Being more than a conquer entails becoming more than you ever imagined you could be. Allowing God to make you great, to carry you to the place of destiny solely reserved for you. As you conquer limitations, you will see yourself moving forward and no longer struggling with some of the minute things that once held you back.

Questions to explore:
*What are the limitations you have placed on yourself?*
*What are the limitations other have tried to place on you?*
*Name one impossible goal you are working towards achieving.*

## Struggling with Lack of Hope

Will it always be like this?

No. The scriptures say Gods plans for your life are for good and not evil, be encouraged that your circumstances are just that. Circumstances are just temporary situations they are not the sum total of your life and does not dictate the outcome of your life. Do not judge the rest of your life based on where you are now. Situations and circumstances are always subject to change; if they determined your future, then your life would be a "hodgepodge" of events and would be unstable. This is not the life that Jesus died for you to have. A life of wholeness, filled with love, joy, and peace is what he sacrificed for.

The bible says for the joy set before him He endured the cross. Jesus endured to reconcile you to God and the joy of a complete relationship with the Father. You can endure when you know the price you are paying now is gaining you something that is priceless. Something that money can't buy, and human hands cannot make happen. God is the only one who can bring up and out the hope that He has placed in your heart.

He is the creator and sustainer of the hope. He can cause the issues you face to come to a good expected end.

Where nothing is missing or out of place, where all is well with your soul. You can endure; you should endure for the end of the thing is better than the beginning.

You endure difficult times by daily pushing forward. You push forward by choosing to do things that help you accomplish your goal; by choosing to live your life despite the circumstances facing you. You endure by choosing a positive attitude and right thinking about your conditions. When your back is against the wall, there is no place to go but forward. Pushing back may frighten you, but it is this act of taking control that will help you to endure what you are facing.

Know that one day the tears will stop, and joy will return. This may seem impossible right now. As you look around you, all you can see the trouble all around and the pain of what has happened to you is still fresh in your heart. Be assured that if you let go of the circumstance that your joy will return to you slowly. How do you let go of the circumstance? It will take time, commitment and a change in your mindset. Let us begin with honesty.

You cannot let go of something until you have truly been honest with yourself about what it is you need to let go. Be brutally honest about the situation currently facing you.

For example, let's say you are going through a rough period in your relationship before you can let go of the pain and stress that comes with this you will have to be honest with yourself and with God about what is really happening. Honesty about your feelings towards your partner, honest about your hurt, honest about your fears (abandonment, etc.), honest with God about what led you to the place you are now. Once you can be honest about where you are at, you will see the situation not from a selfish point of view but a truthful one.

Expressing everything to the point that you feel that you have given God all you know about the situation. For some of you, this will begin as an endless vent, at times it may seem like rambling, and if you are writing this down, it will seem like you have gone mad and the paper may be wet with tears. Yet in the end, it will release so much of what you are dealing with that you would have made room to begin to hear from God. God loves to create something from nothing and take a mess and turn it into a message.

We must do our part by giving Him the raw materials to work with. So, after you have faced the truth about yourself and the situation, then make a commitment, a decision that from this moment on you will change how you think and talk about the situation. The purpose in your heart to let love cover the disappointment.

Learning to forgive often and quickly is an indispensable asset in marriage. Because your husband is not perfect and simply human with issues, stressors, baggage, and tendencies, you will have to make allowances when these are revealed in daily living.

How will you know when the tears are about to stop?

They may not stop for a long time, but they will lessen as you change your perspective of the situation. For example, the loss of a loved one, every time you think of them you may cry, when you stop thinking about your loss. You remember how much you miss them and while thinking about the gift they gave to your life, the blessing they were in the time you had. Think about their legacy, how they touched your life even if it was brief. With every life, there is an impact on others around them. The key for some is to ask the questions: how this person has affected my life, what did they teach me, how can I pass on to others what I have learned.

Perspective has much to do with how we translate experience from one that causes pain or is negative to one that causes pleasure and is positive. Let's use rejection as an example, it can be interpreted as something wrong with us or that there was not a right fit. When you view rejection as something wrong with you, it will cause pain.

Viewing a rejection as helping you avoid entering a relationship, a deal, a job that may not be for you then it becomes a positive tool.

We can stop the tears by trying to go through the process. The process begins with honesty; then purpose in your heart to do the right thing, and lastly change your perspective on the result. This will help take something difficult and place a positive perspective on it.

Questions to explore:
*What is one thing you are willing to let go to embrace something new?*
*How can you protect the hope you have?*
*Name three ways to nurture hope in your life?*

## Struggling with The Enemy in Me

It is easy to fight when you can see the enemy on the outside coming at you. You can see when the enemy is coming at you can make choices to fight or flight. When the enemy is within you, your judgment and therefore conclusions are not clear. The bible says, "the heart is deceitfully wicked, who can know it." We can be deceived by our desires, wrong or poor self-image, by our perceptions of God our fears. In every decision or desire, we have triggers and influences operating that we may not be aware of. Therefore, we are not always making decisions based on the best of information.

A relationship with God and other people who are mature, wise and have our best in mind is essential. The relationship with God will guide you towards His best for your life in every area and will cause you to have and abide in a place of peace and truth. The relationship with others helps your perspective to be balanced out with others and truth to be revealed by having a 360-degree perspective on the issues faced.

You can see the potential for being stuck, blind to your own issues, prideful and in denial without a check from God and others. There will be a round against the "enemy inside of me" resist the urge to believe your own press and not honestly correcting and shaping your decisions.

Do not allow tunnel vision to steal away your ability to be creative and effective. Do not allow yourself to play into wrong thinking or games or change something so that others will feel comfortable in the mediocrity, envy or selfishness.

Questions to explore:
*How has my ego kept me in denial?*
*What are the ways my emotions have clouded my judgment?*
*Whose opinion do I trust and willing to listen to for growth?*

## Struggling to Face your Fears

What do you do when the thing that you were most afraid of ever having to face, finds you and forces you to deal with it? It feels like you are walking merrily along minding your own business when from around the corner comes this giant who hits you in the stomach before you can shout for help, put up your guard or prepare yourself for what is coming.

We all have fears, fear of loss, fear of abandonment, fear of abuse, fear of rejection, fear of disapproval from parents, fear of pain, fear of judgment, fear of shame, fear of being called a fraud and much more. We can sometimes give so much attention to our fears that we live our lives trying to avoid the situations and make decisions based on avoidance of fear instead of faith. When we live also expecting something bad to happen and always talking about it, we are in danger of speaking this negative prophecy into existence.

You have turned the corner only to find your giant facing you. What do you do now? Identify what just happen, call the giant for what it really is, be honest about your feelings, be honest about the situation and do not place unfair judgment and expectations on yourself. This is a counterproductive behavior because it will paralyze you.

If this is something that is occurring to someone you love, separate your past experience with this situation and your fears from the reality of what is going on. The person you love may be dealing with abuse, and you are very sensitive in this area because you were once abused. First, you must acknowledge this is not your experience but someone else, this way you do not rob your loved one from their own unique emotions and need to work this out for themselves. This encounter with a familiar foe may provide an opportunity for you to heal from your past issues but it should not overtake shadow or misconstrue the current issues.

Contain this giant within boundaries set by you. This means a problem with your child, husband or at work should not overtake your life to the point where it impedes or endangers other aspects of your life. It should be kept within boundaries so that you can function with some normalcy while you deal with the issues.

This is important because some issues will take longer to resolve than others, yet in the meantime, you do not want to have to repair every area of your life because of one containable issue. An example if you let problems with one child get so out of hand that you neglect your other children, spouse, and your work, once you have dealt with the child that was causing the issue, you will be left repair the unnecessary damage that may have occurred in the other relationships. You can contain the giant in your life by not involving unnecessarily other people and by continuing as many normal routines, and activities as possible. Sudden changes in your behavior, routines or affections can have a punishing or adverse effect on those who are innocent in your life.

Prepare to conquer this giant with everything you have and know that you hold on to the victory you have by not giving room for this giant to ever show up in your life again. You can protect yourself and insulate against attacks in some very practical ways. You begin to conquer the giant by calling on God the giant slayer to fight on your behalf. You can pray for God to defeat this thing in your life while honestly talking to Him about your emotions, fears, and hopes.

When you have the tool or instructions you need to defeat this giant then you are required to go act this out. It is like having a leak and taking the putty and sealing the leaking. You had the tool; the instruction was to apply and once you made the hole was sealed, and the leak stopped. Next, you have to maintain the victory every day, by changing the way you think about the issues, do not meditate on it in your mind.

When thoughts about the issue come up, change your mind on purpose, get up physically, move, talk about something else, quote the scriptures related to your victory. Tell yourself about the positive outcome you have.

Questions to explore:
*What are the fears holding you back from change?*
*How can you be more proactive in facing uncertainty and less reactive?*
*What are the thoughts that take the most mental and emotional energy?*

## Struggling Let Go of Victim Mentality

Circumstances out of your control may take place at times in your life that make you feel or experience the pain of being a victim. As a person that has suffered loss, a bad circumstance or a crime committed against, you are justified in seeing yourself as someone who was victimized. How you see yourself and what you say about yourself can either help you heal or keep you stuck in the way of thinking that will continue the reliving of the pain. There is a difference in perspective from someone who was victimized and someone who describes and sees themselves as a victim, year after year.

This difference in perspective causes some to be a person who was victimized to take steps to gain healing and victory over the circumstance or pain. Some either through anger, depression or denial choose to remain a victim and stuck in the same place emotionally year after year. This may seem harsh because no one chooses to be a victim. That is true, no one chooses to be victimized, not seeking healing when you are able to is a choice to stay in the position, emotions, and mindset of someone who is a victim.

It is not the event that determines how you see it; you are in control of how you choose to interpret what happens and how you define yourself considering what happened. The label of the victim is often applied when someone is reliving the pain of momentary experience, over and over; so much so that the situation seems to resurrect with the mere mention of a word, familiar smell or a thought. This can also be a sign suffering from Post-Traumatic Stress Disorder (PTSD). If this is the case its time to seek professional help to begin the healing process.

There is a healing process that we must engage to properly recover from a traumatic experience or a loss. When we have gone through that process, it will change our perspective if we let it. For some people their perspective of life, themselves and God will either cause them to move into the winner's circle as a victor or stand on the sidelines as a victim. Perspective defined is how we interpret what we are looking at or experiencing. Our perspective is usually filtered through the lens of our past experiences, values, and beliefs. Perspective allows us to sort through and categorize the vast amount of information that our senses take in every day.

This wonderful tool called perspective allows for a diversity of thinking and experiences in individuals. Perspective can also have a negative effect if we apply it in a negative fashion.

For example, if from your perspective on life is it:
- Full of problems waiting to happen.
- Life is one big out of control set of circumstances.
- Life is controlled by chance.
- Life is good and bad events, and you hope for more of the good than bad.
- Life is hard, and you can just hope to get through ok.
- Life is what you alone make into.
- Life is god getting back at us for something we did.
- Life is the chaos that happens between birth and death.

These are pessimistic, and punitive perspectives on life are what will cause someone to remain in the mindset of being a victim and not a victor. Making a conscious effort to choose to think differently allows you to take back your power and control.

To move into the victor's circle in life, you must change your perspective, which in turn will change your mindset. The difference between seeing life and difficult times as opportunities or stepping stones will mean living life on purpose and not by chance. A life lived on purpose will have meaningful, tangible and useful results. A life lived by chance is like throwing sand into the wind. It will be scattered, have not effect other than to possibly become an irritant in someone's eye.

See the purpose in your pain and make it work towards pushing you forward in life rather than making you stagnate or continuously struggling; cause obstacles to become stepping stones by succeeding despite them. Let God guide you and lead you so that you can cherish, and experience life rather than just get by in life. Let God change your perspective by giving you His eternal, global and timeless perspective. Revealing to you what each earthly step or experience looks like in the light of eternity.

## Struggling to Know Who You Are

The way to overcome the intimidation, influence and brainwashing of others is to know who you are and stand assured in that knowledge. Knowing who you are, being comfortable with and confident in yourself will help you to overcome the need to please others. Knowledge of oneself helps to keep you on the path that God has for your life. You will find on your journey towards your destiny that well-intended, loving even close friends will try to influence you to do things their way. They will try to convince you, if you are not careful, to go their way, to take on their mission as your own. Although well intended their mission may not be your mission.

Whatever your role or calling be sure that you are following the lead and influence of God's Spirit in your life. It would be a tragedy to follow the lead of another human being that is limited and cannot see the whole picture or know what your full potential is. God who created you knows the unique gifts stored in you. God knows the best environment for the building and training in your gifts. Following the leading of the God's Spirit will help to ensure you get to the place where you are supposed to be. Following the God's Spirit will ensure you take advantage of the opportunities which God has created for you.

We all have a unique calling in God, some of us are called to be in the forefront, and some are called to be supporters of those in the forefront. Whether you are called in a starring role or a supportive role, remember that the movie cannot be made without you. Remember there is a reward for supporting as well as lead actors. Remember that in God we are all equal, yet our roles can be very different.

## Strong Women Win

Get noticed, take on the big risk and test yourself. Stop being afraid to fail. Take calculated risk, build in some supports, know you have options and go for it. Manage your career as you manage everything else in your life. Do not leave it up to someone else to decide your fate. Do the things you will excel at, focus on your strength, and make them produce greater results.

Do not make quick or emotional decisions, wait, because in waiting you can collect information, sort out the real from the fake and not get set up by others. Everything looks different in the light of day; therefore, wait, consult and weigh options before making any life-altering decisions.

**Summary**

We have examined many reasons for the way we think and react, let's recap some:

*You do it because it works.*

No one would keep on doing something that did not produce results. Whether people judge your reasons as good or bad, you do what you do because it works. You use your influence over others because it works.

You use anger or manipulation with people in your life because it gets you what you want in the moment. We use sex because it works (often temporarily) to get what we want. Some will make excuses or give reasons for using a harmful method or means because of the end result. The consequences of these are broken relationships, guilt, shame and becoming stuck in the same patterns repeatedly. Breaking the pattern of harmful behavior begins with recognize and admitting that it works in the short term but is dangerous in the long term.

*You do because it is rewarding.*

You have benefited from the public persona financially and in your career. It has gotten you the things you wanted out of life, so you consider it a good investment. You took a risk, and it paid off very well, as you kept doing more you kept getting what you wanted.

*Feels good*

If something feels bad, our instinct is to no longer do it, but if it feels good, we seek it again. We seek pleasure from foods we eat, relationships, activities, and indulgences. The reward for seeking pleasure is getting it. Then we become addicted to the pleasure feelings and thoughts, and we go after it again and again; forsaking everything that matters for the moments of pleasure, which has become so powerful in our life.

*Satisfies ego*

This is when we are likely to sit back and say, "look at what I have accomplished". Thinking because of all that you have done you are entitled to certain things regardless of the cost to someone else. Feeling good about your accomplishments is healthy, yet when out of balance it becomes pride, entitlement, self-righteousness and leads to putting down or belittling of others. The ego wants the world to know about every good deed done and how wonderful you are. Once the compliments come in it desires more and will do anything to get more. An ego seeking acknowledgment works hand in hand with a love-starved heart.

*It's all you know*

Doing something because it the only way were taught sounds like this "I do what I do the way I do it because it is all I know. It's how I was raised; the role models in my life did it the same way. It's the only trick I know, and I good at it". When reacting in a certain way is familiar and almost second nature, there is no right, or wrong judgment involved it is "just because." Without rhyme or reason, we react instantly. This is a result of lack of exposure to other options causing a reversion to what is familiar. To break this pattern requires learning how to respond instead of react, this is being in control of when and how you take action or make a statement.

*Comfortable*

"My attitude, my way, fits like a glove. I wear my public persona well, and I can work it any which way I choose. So why change something that is so naturally tailored made for me".

This is the type of person who feels everyone else exist to adjust to them rather than change. They do not care about the discomfort of others is not their concern.

*It's so big it's out of your control*

The dream came true and you were not prepared for the reality. "It began as a childhood dream, a what if, or someday I will, thought. Now the success seems overnight; it has taken off faster than I can wrap my mind around. It is growing every day, and a simple dream has now brought me fame and money that is overwhelming. I do not know what to do, and I am still playing ketchup to get a grasp of what is taking place. No one prepared me for this kind of success. I do not know how to start to gain control".

*Afraid of the consequences*

When your decisions have lasting impact on your loves ones or those working for you. "So many people are impacted by the decisions I make. With expectations high, there is no room for failure and nowhere to retreat. What I am doing has not been done before; to quit, change the course or let it go will shatter the hopes of others and would make people mad at me. I do not like being thought badly of or making others mad at me."

*Afraid of changing and not being in control*
"I like my life most days, I am in control and rarely taken by surprise. Although things are not perfect, and some choices are unhealthy, I am in control. I pride myself on being in control, thinking way ahead has gotten me this far. To change course would mean not been in control and introducing the unknown in my life that I am not ready. I will take the sure thing over the maybe any day. I will rather be safe, and little miserable than have no idea what is coming next and fully miserable".

Strong women, they are often balancing a full-time job, family and other commitments while trying to pursue their dreams. How can someone manage all the above and do it well? You can manage it all. They key is to become a good planner and write everything down, this will save you time, money and energy. Sounds simple, yet so many entrepreneurs will lose valuable money-making ideas because they have not taken the time to write down the idea when it comes to them.

Writing things down has another added benefit, it will help to keep you organized and on track with your workload. In the frenzy of activity, we lose track of some of the smaller tasks and put off some vital contacts or mailings that need to be attended to. Write down a task that you are in the progress of doing, and tasks that must be done later. This will help you to make plans on how you will spend your time during the week. Balancing work, friendships and family obligations will take preparation and planning time to execute your daily tasks well. The more you can track what you are doing, and why you are doing it, the more productive you will become.

As you continue to grow, and a decision will have to be made to get better and not bitter. That you are not going to spend another day in bed, hurting, regretting, angry, sad or anyone one of the many emotions we go through when we are having a pity party. Begin with the decision, then move into taking action, get up, get moving, and you will have great success. You have accomplished a goal, and you are feeling a part of you that was oppressed, and quiet is now awakened. You ride on that accomplishment until "pow" un-expectantly you are hit hard by a reminder of the problem or situation that you are dealing with. You find yourself breaking down once again, crying and feeling like the step forward you took no longer counts because once again you were pushed back four steps.

Do not stop there. Release the tears, allow the feelings, take in what just happened and then get focused once again and get back on the path to achieving your goals, towards healing and a better tomorrow. For every day you spend sitting and rehearsing the same scenarios one more day that could have been used to help you move forward in your life. Every day is an investment in the future; when you see that today is really about what you will be tomorrow, then you are less likely to waste it.

## About the Author Page

Gessy Martinez is the author of several books, an award-winning public speaker and trainer, mother, licensed minister, Business and Personal Development Coach and Licensed Professional Counselor. Blending skills in management, supervising, planning, development, and experience as a parent of young adults, teen and school age children and President of Aspire and Reach for More, LLC. Familiar with struggle and passionate about helping others through encouragement, training and counseling.

To connect with her visit the website:
aspireandreachformore.com

*If you enjoyed this book, I would love to hear your thoughts about! Stop by Amazon leave a review or Facebook and leave a message.*

**Other books by this author**
The Weekend Entrepreneur
The Mommy Entrepreneur
52 Reasons to Live: Why Greatness Refuses to Die

www.ingramcontent.com/pod-product-compliance
Lightning Source LLC
Chambersburg PA
CBHW071514040426
42444CB00008B/1640